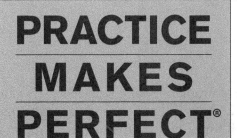

PRACTICE MAKES PERFECT®

Writing Japanese Kana

Rita L. Lampkin and Osamu Hoshino

Mc Graw Hill Education

New York Chicago San Francisco Athens London Madrid
Mexico City Milan New Delhi Singapore Sydney Toronto

About the Authors

Rita L. Lampkin is a graduate of Brigham Young University–Hawaii Campus and a veteran of some thirty years teaching Japanese and English as a Second Language, having served as a missionary in Japan and another year as a full-time English instructor for Nippon Electric Company. Her experience also includes three years both teaching and developing materials for intensive courses in Hawaii. She developed and taught a course in basic Japanese for employees of Disneyland in Anaheim, California, and spent over eighteen years teaching at Mt. San Antonio College in Walnut, California, having pioneered the Japanese program there. Other publications include *Japanese Verbs and Essentials of Grammar, Easy Japanese Crossword Puzzles, The Japanese Way* (co-author), and numerous other works for both Japanese and ESL.

Osamu Hoshino also graduated from BYU–Hawaii Campus, where he and Mrs. Lampkin first collaborated in teaching Japanese and developing course materials. He then moved to BYU's main campus at Provo, Utah, where he received an MPA while teaching Japanese at BYU's Missionary Training Center. A native of Japan, he has also taught ESL in his home country. He has since taken American citizenship and is a past Director of the Utah Department of Economic Development. He currently works as an economic development consultant for several western states.

2 3 4 5 6 7 8 9 10 QVS/QVS 19 18 17 16 15 14

ISBN   978-0-07-182798-0
MHID   0-07-182798-6

Library of Congress Control Number 2013934654

McGraw-Hill Education, the McGraw-Hill Education logo, Practice Makes Perfect, and related trade dress are trademarks or registered trademarks of McGraw-Hill Education and/or its affiliates in the United States and other countries and may not be used without written permission. All other trademarks are the property of their respective owners. McGraw-Hill Education is not associated with any product or vendor mentioned in this book.

McGraw-Hill Education products are available at special quantity discounts to use as premiums and sales promotions or for use in corporate training programs. To contact a representative, please visit the Contact Us pages at www.mhprofessional.com.

This book is printed on acid-free paper.

Writing Practice Grid

To access the online writing practice grid for this book, please follow these instructions:

1. Go to mhprofessional.com/mediacenter.
2. Enter this book's ISBN: 978-0-07-182798-0 and select the Find Product button.
3. Enter your e-mail address to receive a link to the downloadable files.

Contents

PART TWO

PART THREE

Introduction

This practical workbook is for all students of Japanese who want to learn the basic phonetic writing systems in use by the Japanese. This workbook is a self-contained course, which can be used both for independent study or in the classroom. It can also serve as an ideal supplement to any basic conversation course in Japanese.

Both the hiragana and katakana sections of this workbook provide plenty of practice in writing characters, words, and sentences. In addition, each section concludes with practice exercises and self-tests. After these sections you'll find a complete review of hiragana and katakana for additional practice.

At the back of the book are several useful appendices, including complete hiragana and katakana charts as well as answers and translations to the practice exercises and self-tests.

Practice Makes Perfect: Writing Japanese Kana combines a systematic approach with ample practice and the reinforcement necessary to master both reading and writing hiragana and katakana.

Overview of the three Japanese writing systems

There are three kinds of characters involved in writing Japanese:

- ◆ **KANJI**
- ◆ **KATAKANA**
- ◆ **HIRAGANA**

1. **KANJI** is a set of ideographs and pictographs borrowed originally from the Chinese and adapted to fit the Japanese language.

   Each *KANJI* character carries a specific meaning and may be pronounced several different ways, depending on its use. There are over 1800 *KANJI* in common use, plus a good number of less frequently used or archaic characters.

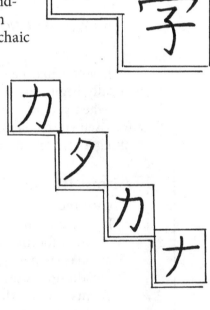

2. **KATAKANA** is a strictly phonetic system. That is, each character represents a particular sound, with no inherent meaning.

   KATAKANA is used to write, as closely as the limited Japanese sound system will allow, words and names of foreign origin. It is also used to place emphasis on or call attention to a particular word or phrase and is used liberally in advertising.

   There are 46 basic characters in the *KATAKANA* system, plus a number of "combination characters" (contracted characters) and "sound change characters."

3. **HIRAGANA** is also strictly phonetic, has the same number of characters as the *KATAKANA* system, and represents the same set of sounds. The only difference between the two systems is in their use.

   HIRAGANA is used to write particles, verb endings, conjunctions, etc.—all the words or parts of words that are not represented in *KATAKANA* or *KANJI*.

   The two sets of phonetic characters (*HIRAGANA* and *KATAKANA*) are known collectively as *KANA*.

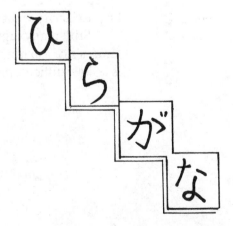

Since the *KANA* symbols are strictly phonetic, they may be used to write any word for which *KANJI* is not customarily used, or for which the *KANJI* is not known to the writer. For these purposes, *HIRAGANA* is ordinarily used, rather than *KATAKANA*.

Japanese children usually are taught first *HIRAGANA* and then *KATAKANA*, while concurrently studying some of the simpler *KANJI*. The same order will be used in this course as well.

The three Japanese writing systems—*HIRAGANA*, *KATAKANA*, and *KANJI*—are used in combination with each other, as shown in the following example sentence:

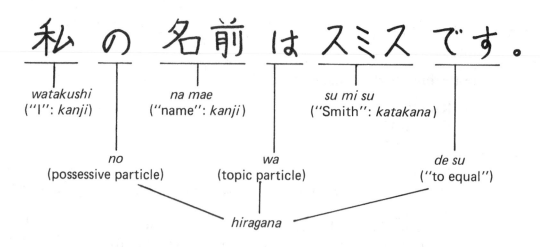

WATAKUSHI NO NAMAE WA SUMISU DESU.   =   My name is Smith.

Japanese may be written horizontally, from left to right, like English, or from top to bottom vertically, beginning at the right side of the page, and moving toward the left. There are rare occasions when you may see it written horizontally from right to left. On a vehicle, for example, an advertisement or identification will be written from the front of the vehicle towards the rear, making it read left to right on one side and right to left on the other.

About Rōmaji (The Roman Alphabet)

Over the last century several systems of romanization have been developed to represent the Japanese sound system. There have even been attempts at a permanent substitution of *RŌMAJI* for the much more difficult *KANJI* system, although there has never been enough popular support to bring the idea to reality. One of the major problems in making such a substitution is the fact that the Japanese sound system is extremely limited, making homonyms—words that sound alike but have different meanings—the rule, rather than the exception. Since *KANJI* characters illustrate the meaning of the words they represent, they help to clarify what is being written.

Still, many Japanese conversation texts use one or another of the various *RŌMAJI* systems, since learning Japanese as a second language by way of *KANA* and *KANJI* exclusively is a slow, difficult process.

PART ONE

Hiragana no gojūon

The 50 sounds of Hiragana

The word *GOJŪON* literally means "50 sounds," although the modern system of *KANA* actually consists of only 46 symbols.

Note that the characters in the chart below represent syllables, rather than individual sounds as in the Roman alphabet. For this reason the set of symbols is called a SYLLABARY.

A syllable in the Japanese system may be a single vowel sound (*A, I, U, E,* or *O)* or a consonant-vowel combination, such as *KA* or *TSU* or *CHI*. The only exception is the soft consonant *N'* (ん), which is also considered a single syllable.

Note also that this chart is presented in vertical order, beginning in the upper right-hand corner and moving downward and across the page toward the left. This is the order in which words are given in a *KANA* dictionary, just as words are given in A-B-C order in a dictionary using the Roman alphabet. When you memorize these characters, you should memorize them in order.

Begin here. ↓

わ WA	ら RA	や YA	ま MA	は HA	な NA	た TA	さ SA	か KA	あ A
	り RI		み MI	ひ HI	に NI	ち CHI	し SHI	き KI	い I
	る RU	ゆ YU	む MU	ふ FU	ぬ NU	つ TSU	す SU	く KU	う U
	れ RE		め ME	へ HE	ね NE	て TE	せ SE	け KE	え E
を (W)O	ろ RO	よ YO	も MO	ほ HO	の NO	と TO	そ SO	こ KO	お O
ん N'									

This chart is given in machine-made characters in Appendix A.

Writing Kana characters

The exercises on the following pages are intended not only to help you learn to recognize and write the *HIRAGANA* characters but also to help you to develop good penmanship. Keep the following points in mind as you carry out the exercises presented.

1. For the purpose of writing practice, each character is presented within a square. Notice that the character is always more or less CENTERED IN ITS SQUARE. In normal circumstances, of course, the squares are absent; but the characters should still be spaced as if written in a row or column of squares. Closer spacing of the characters may make your writing difficult to read.

2. In English and many other languages, it is considered appropriate to slant letters or to add extra curlicues and swashes, according to the handwriting style of the individual. In Japanese, however, THE CHARACTERS SHOULD BE WRITTEN AS SHOWN, UPRIGHT and with no more slant, curl, or swash than is shown for each character. Slanting a *KANA* character may make it look like some other character and become difficult to read.

3. You should realize that *KANA* and *KANJI* were originally created when brush-and-ink was the normal writing medium. The brush was held upright in the hand, rather than at an angle as a pen or pencil would be used. It may help your penmanship if you TRY HOLDING YOUR PEN UPRIGHT as you write the characters.

upright, like a brush

4. Pay careful attention to the STROKE ORDER and STROKE DIRECTION indicated by the numbers and arrows, as these are essential to correct formation of each character. Note that basic stroke order moves from left to right and top to bottom, although there are occasional variations. Also, horizontal strokes are ordinarily written before vertical strokes.

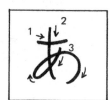

5. TAKE YOUR TIME with these exercises. Don't rush through them, but use them to develop good writing habits and penmanship.

First, **TRACE** each character several times, paying strict attention to stroke order and direction. Then carefully draw the character in the blank squares. Take your time. Develop good habits NOW.

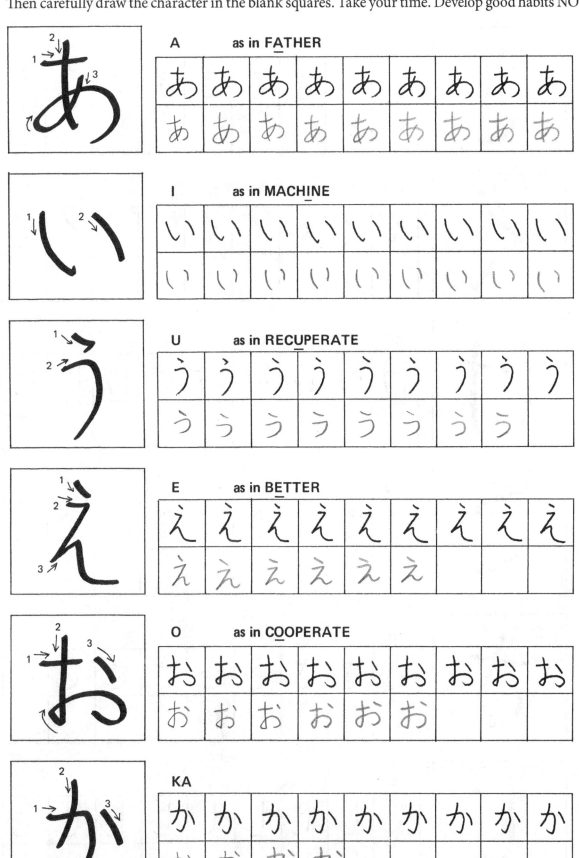

A   as in F**A**THER

I   as in MACH**I**NE

U   as in REC**U**PERATE

E   as in B**E**TTER

O   as in C**O**OPERATE

KA

First, **TRACE** each character several times, paying strict attention to stroke order and direction. Then carefully draw the character in the blank squares. Take your time. Develop good habits NOW.

KI   like "key"

き き き き き き き き き
き き

KU

く く く く く く く く く
く く く

KE   as in **KEPT**

け け け け け け け け け
け け け

KO

こ こ こ こ こ こ こ こ こ
こ こ

SA

さ さ さ さ さ さ さ さ さ
さ さ

SHI   like "she"

し し し し し し し し し
し し

First, **TRACE** each character several times, paying strict attention to stroke order and direction. Then carefully draw the character in the blank squares. Take your time. Develop good habits NOW.

SU

SE   as in **SETTLE**

SO

TA

CHI   as in **CHEEK**

TSU

First, **TRACE** each character several times, paying strict attention to stroke order and direction. Then carefully draw the character in the blank squares. Take your time. Develop good habits NOW.

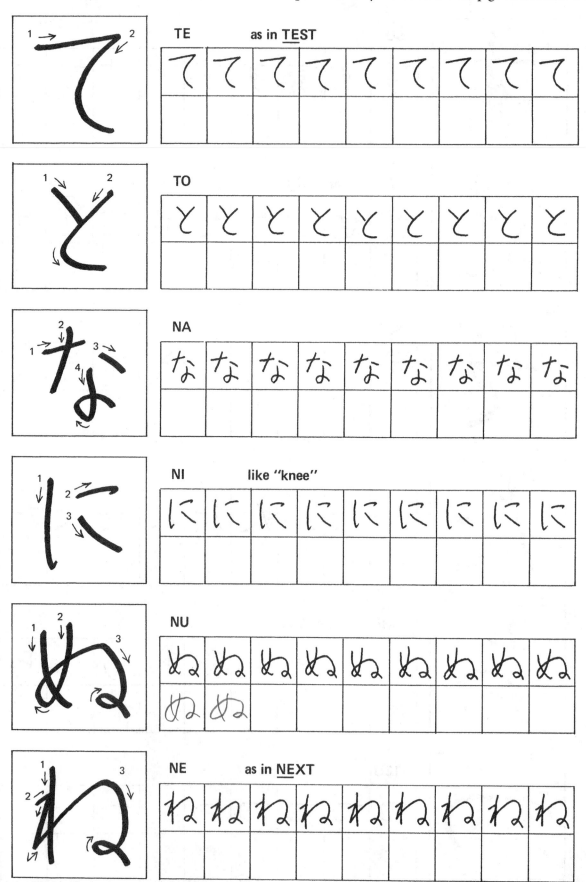

TE   as in <u>TE</u>ST

TO

NA

NI   like "knee"

NU

NE   as in <u>NE</u>XT

First, **TRACE** each character several times, paying strict attention to stroke order and direction.
Then carefully draw the character in the blank squares. Take your time. Develop good habits NOW.

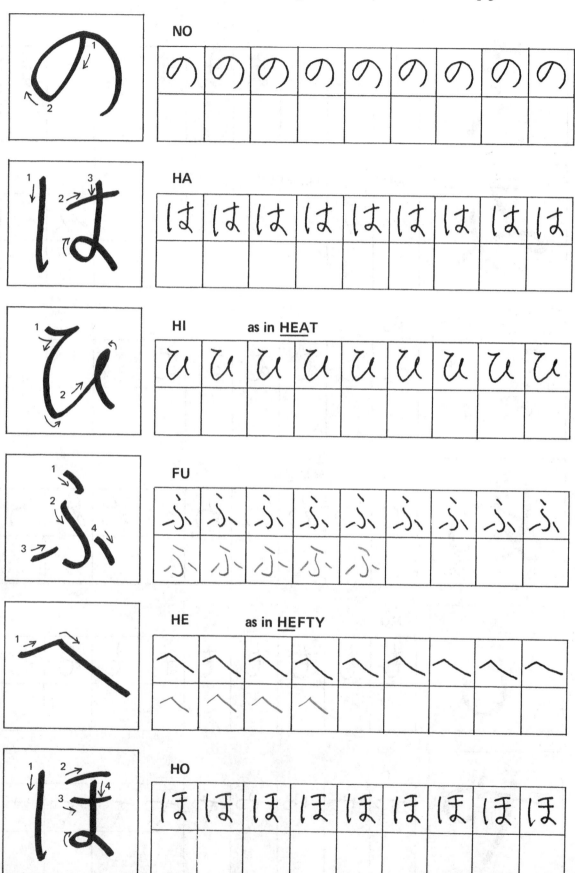

NO

HA

HI   as in **HEAT**

FU

HE   as in **HEFTY**

HO

First, **TRACE** each character several times, paying strict attention to stroke order and direction. Then carefully draw the character in the blank squares. Take your time. Develop good habits NOW.

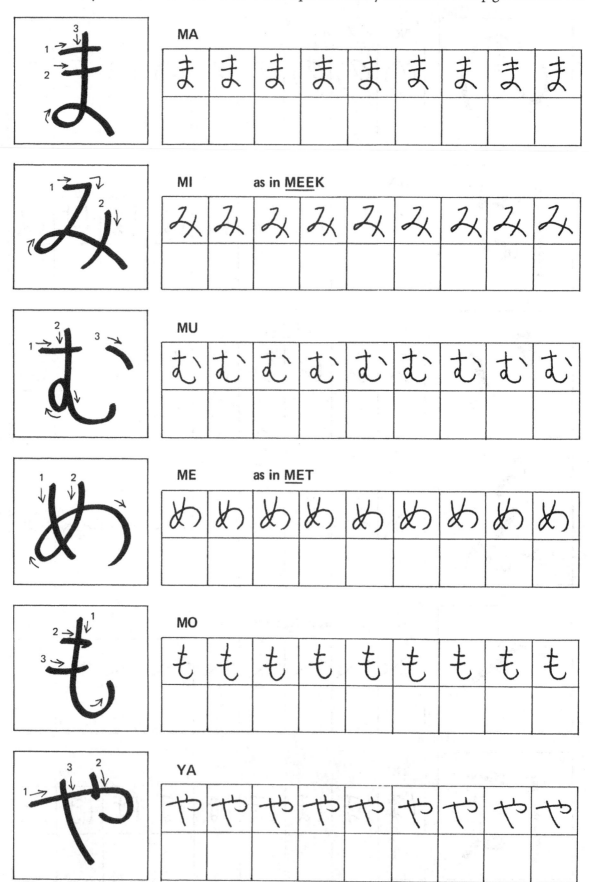

MA

ま ま ま ま ま ま ま ま ま

MI   as in <u>MEEK</u>

み み み み み み み み み

MU

む む む む む む む む む

ME   as in <u>MET</u>

め め め め め め め め め

MO

も も も も も も も も も

YA

や や や や や や や や や

First, **TRACE** each character several times, paying strict attention to stroke order and direction.
Then carefully draw the character in the blank squares. Take your time. Develop good habits NOW.

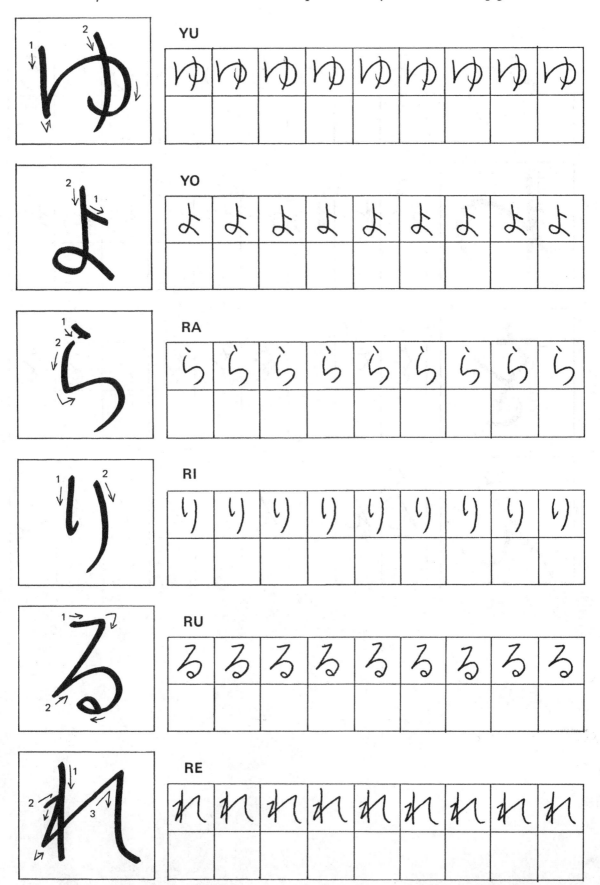

YU

YO

RA

RI

RU

RE

First, **TRACE** each character several times, paying strict attention to stroke order and direction. Then carefully draw the character in the blank squares. Take your time. Develop good habits NOW.

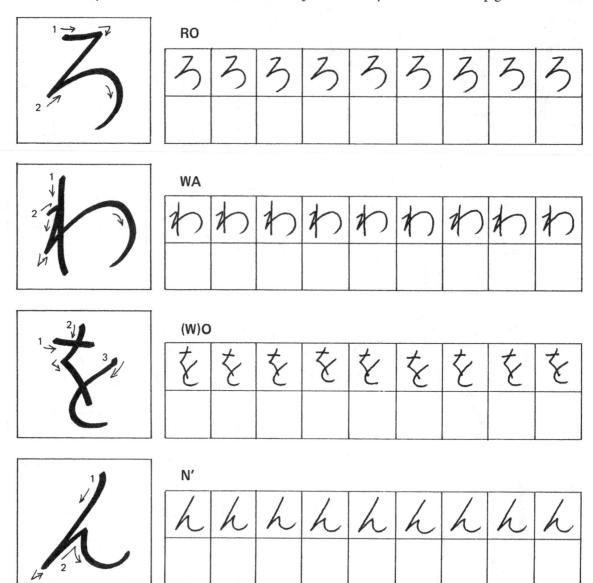

RO

WA

(W)O

N'

Voiced vs. voiceless consonants

Besides the basic sounds of the *GOJŪON*, there are variations of some of these syllables, made by changing a VOICELESS consonant to a VOICED consonant.

To illustrate what is meant by VOICED and VOICELESS consonants, first put your hand on your throat so that your palm is against the Adam's apple, as in the illustration at right. Now, say the following consonant sounds (just the sound of the letter, not the letter's name):

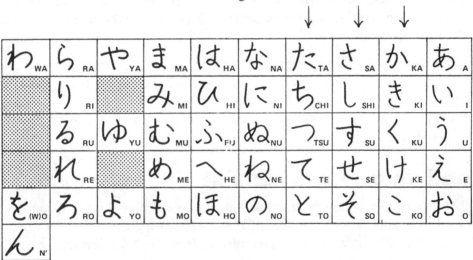

/G/	(as in GOOD)
/Z/	(as in ZIPPER)
/D/	(as in DARLING)

Notice the vibration that you feel when you pronounce each of these VOICED consonants, so named because they are made by vibrating the vocal cords.

Now pronounce the VOICELESS counterparts of the same consonant sounds:

/K/ (as in KOALA)   /S/ (as in SOCKS)   /T/ (as in TAPE)

Notice the lack of vibration from the vocal cords when these sounds are pronounced. Notice also that there is no other difference in the way each pair of sounds is pronounced: /G/ is the voiced counterpart of /K/, /Z/ is the voiced counterpart of /S/, and /D/ is the voiced counterpart of /T/. The mouth, lips, and tongue are in the same position for each pair; only the vocalization is different.

Now take a look at the *GOJŪON* chart again:

				↓		↓		↓		
わ WA	ら RA	や YA	ま MA	は HA	な NA	た TA	さ SA	か KA	あ A
	り RI		み MI	ひ HI	に NI	ち CHI	し SHI	き KI	い I
	る RU	ゆ YU	む MU	ふ FU	ぬ NU	つ TSU	す SU	く KU	う U
	れ RE		め ME	へ HE	ね NE	て TE	せ SE	け KE	え E
を (W)O	ろ RO	よ YO	も MO	ほ HO	の NO	と TO	そ SO	こ KO	お O
ん N'									

The arrows indicate three columns of syllables that begin with VOICELESS CONSONANTS. These VOICELESS CONSONANTS can be changed to VOICED CONSONANTS by the use of a symbol called *NIGORI* or *TEN-TEN* (meaning "point-point"), placed to the upper right of the voiceless character, as in the chart on the next page.

た TA	だ DA	さ SA	ざ ZA	か KA	が GA
ち CHI	ぢ JI	し SHI	じ JI	き KI	ぎ GI
つ TSU	づ ZU	す SU	ず ZU	く KU	ぐ GU
て TE	で DE	せ SE	ぜ ZE	け KE	げ GE
と TO	ど DO	そ SO	ぞ ZO	こ KO	ご GO

See how *KA* (か) becomes *GA* (が), *SA* (さ) becomes *ZA* (ざ), *TA* (た) becomes *DA* (だ), etc.

Notes

1. Reason would tell us that the sound /SH/, as in the syllable *SHI* (し), when voiced, would become /ZH/, as in the words "measure" and "treasure." However, the /ZH/ sound does not exist in Japanese. The consonant sound represented in the character じ is /J/ as in "John" and "joke."

2. The syllable *CHI* (ち), when voiced, becomes *JI*, the same syllable represented by the character じ . When writing in *KANA*, remember that じ is the character most often used to represent the syllable *JI*. ぢ is used only rarely, and under particular circumstances. For the purposes of the beginner, it is best to use the character じ unless specifically instructed otherwise.

3. Notice that both ず and づ represent the syllable *ZU*. The character used most often for this syllable is ず , the other being used only rarely and under particular circumstances. Again, for the beginner, it is best to use the character ず unless specifically instructed otherwise. (Appendix B includes some common words that call for ぢ and づ instead of じ and ず .)

Voiced and voiceless bilabials

A BILABIAL is a sound made with the lips touching each other. Japanese contains three such bilabials— /M/, /B/, and /P/. The syllables *MA*, *MI*, *MU*, *ME*, and *MO* are included in the basic *GOJŪON* chart. The other bilabials are represented in *HIRAGANA* and romanization as follows:

ば BA	ぱ PA
び BI	ぴ PI
ぶ BU	ぷ PU
べ BE	ぺ PE
ぼ BO	ぽ PO

Notice that the voiced syllables *BA*, *BI*, *BU*, *BE*, and *BO* are represented by the characters for *HA*, *HI*, *FU*, *HE*, and *HO*, accompanied by the usual *NIGORI* points.

The voiceless bilabial syllables *PA*, *PI*, *PU*, *PE*, and *PO* are the same basic characters, accompanied by a small circle, called *MARU* (meaning "circle") or *HANDAKU*.

Use the following exercises to learn to write the voiced and *HANDAKU* characters, paying careful attention to stroke order and direction as shown. Again, DO NOT RUSH these exercises; instead, draw the characters carefully in order to develop good penmanship and correct writing habits.

First, **TRACE** each character several times, paying strict attention to stroke order and direction. Then carefully draw the character in the blank squares. Take your time. Develop good habits NOW.

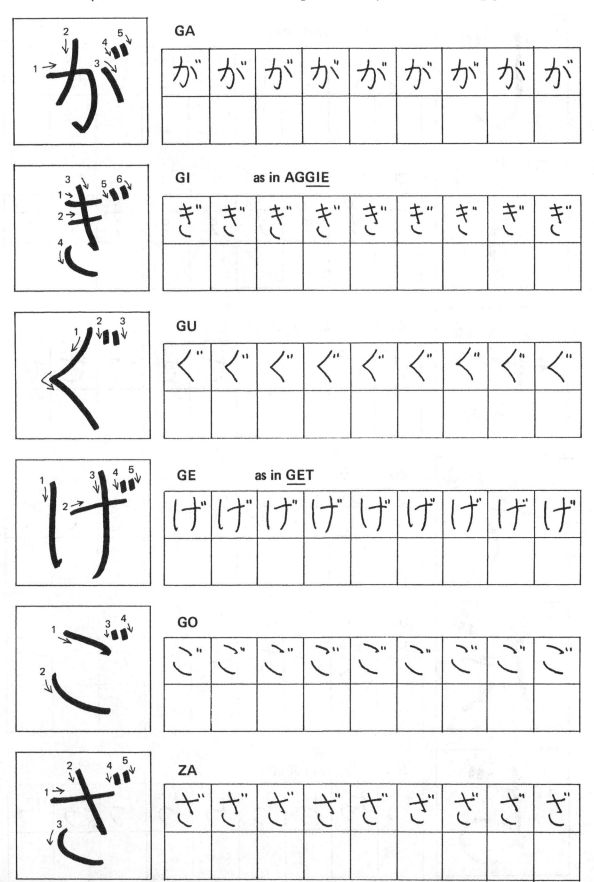

GA

GI   as in AG**GI**E

GU

GE   as in **GE**T

GO

ZA

First, **TRACE** each character several times, paying strict attention to stroke order and direction. Then carefully draw the character in the blank squares. Take your time. Develop good habits NOW.

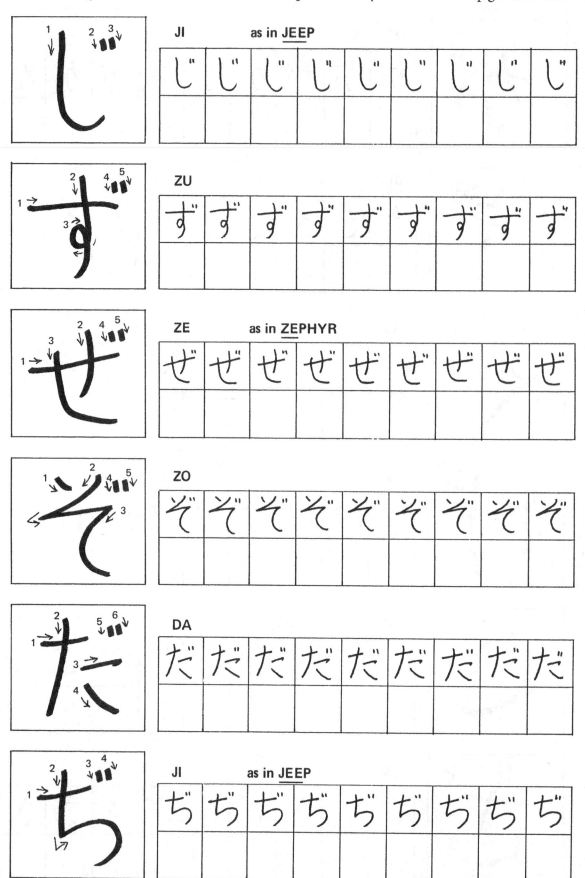

JI   as in <u>JE</u>EP

ZU

ZE   as in <u>ZE</u>PHYR

ZO

DA

JI   as in <u>JE</u>EP

First, **TRACE** each character several times, paying strict attention to stroke order and direction. Then carefully draw the character in the blank squares. Take your time. Develop good habits NOW.

ZU

づ づ づ づ づ づ づ づ づ

DE   as in <u>DE</u>BT

て て て て て て て て て

DO

ど ど ど ど ど ど ど ど ど

BA

ば ば ば ば ば ば ば ば ば

BI   like "BEE"

び び び び び び び び び

BU

ぶ ぶ ぶ ぶ ぶ ぶ ぶ ぶ ぶ

First, **TRACE** each character several times, paying strict attention to stroke order and direction. Then carefully draw the character in the blank squares. Take your time. Develop good habits NOW.

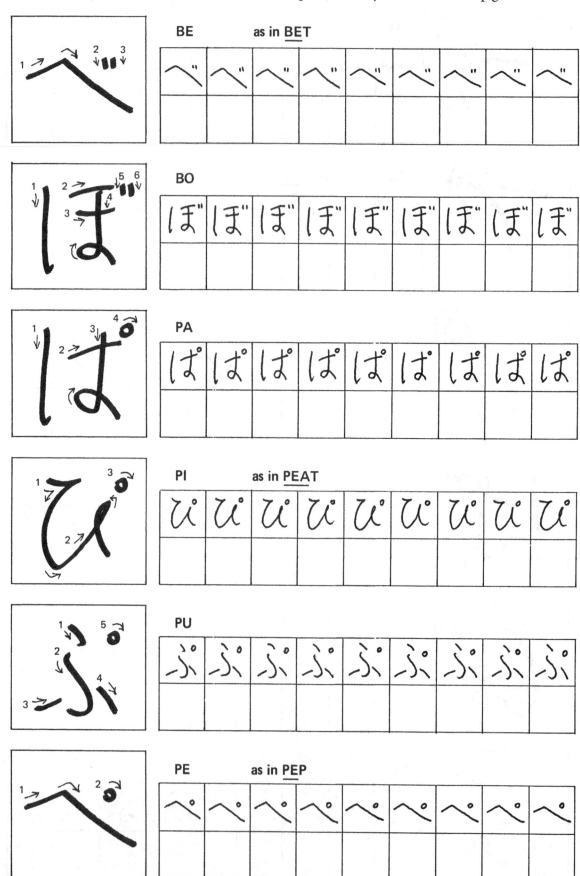

BE   as in **BE**T

BO

PA

PI   as in **PE**AT

PU

PE   as in **PE**P

First, **TRACE** each character several times, paying strict attention to stroke order and direction. Then carefully draw the character in the blank squares. Take your time. Develop good habits NOW.

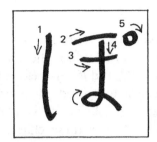

PO

ぽ	ぽ	ぽ	ぽ	ぽ	ぽ	ぽ	ぽ	ぽ

Combination characters (contracted syllables)

Take a look at the *GOJŪON* chart at right, particularly the characters in bold script. When these characters are combined with a smaller version of the characters for *YA* (や), *YU* (ゆ), and *YO* (よ) (indicated by the arrow), they form what are called COMBINATION CHARACTERS, as shown in the chart below.

わ WA	ら RA	や YA	ま MA	は HA	な NA	た TA	さ SA	か KA	あ A
	り RI		み MI	ひ HI	に NI	ち CHI	し SHI	き KI	い I
	る RU	ゆ YU	む MU	ふ FU	ぬ NU	つ TSU	す SU	く KU	う U
	れ RE		め ME	へ HE	ね NE	て TE	せ SE	け KE	え E
を (W)O	ろ RO	よ YO	も MO	ほ HO	の NO	と TO	そ SO	こ KO	お O
ん N'		↑							

This chart is given in machine-made characters in Appendix A.

きゃ KYA	しゃ SHA	ちゃ CHA	にゃ NYA	ひゃ HYA	みゃ MYA	りゃ RYA
きゅ KYU	しゅ SHU	ちゅ CHU	にゅ NYU	ひゅ HYU	みゅ MYU	りゅ RYU
きょ KYO	しょ SHO	ちょ CHO	にょ NYO	ひょ HYO	みょ MYO	りょ RYO

This chart is given in machine-made characters in Appendix A.

These combined characters have the value of one syllable each, as compared with two separate syllables when the characters are written the same size, separately. Note the differences in the following examples:

SHIYA "field of vision"	しや	vs.	*SHA* "gauze"	しゃ
KIYU "imaginary fears"	きゆ	vs.	*KYU* "sphere" "globe"	きゅ
RIYOKU "greed"	りよく	vs.	*RYOKUCHA* "green tea"	りょくちゃ

Of course, the voiceless combination characters also have voiced and bilabialized counterparts, represented as before by the accompanying *NIGORI* and *HANDAKU*, as shown in the following chart:

ぎゃ GYA	じゃ JA	ぢゃ JA	びゃ BYA	ぴゃ PYA
ぎゅ GYU	じゅ JU	ぢゅ JU	びゅ BYU	ぴゅ PYU
ぎょ GYO	じょ JO	ぢょ JO	びょ BYO	ぴょ PYO

This chart is given in machine-made characters in Appendix A.

Note that there are two sets of characters for the sounds *JA, JU,* and *JO.* As before, the characters used most often are じゃ, じゅ, and じょ. It is best to use these characters unless otherwise instructed.

Use the following exercises to learn to write the combination characters, paying careful attention, as always, to stroke order and direction as shown. DO NOT RUSH. Use these exercises to develop good writing habits and penmanship.

First, **TRACE** each character several times, then carefully draw the character in the blank squares.

First, **TRACE** each character several times, paying strict attention to stroke order and direction. Then carefully draw the character in the blank squares. Take your time. Develop good habits NOW.

GYU

ぎゅ	ぎゅ	ぎゅ	ぎゅ	ぎゅ	ぎゅ

GYO

ぎょ	ぎょ	ぎょ	ぎょ	ぎょ	ぎょ

SHA

しゃ	しゃ	しゃ	しゃ	しゃ	しゃ

SHU

しゅ	しゅ	しゅ	しゅ	しゅ	しゅ

SHO

しょ	しょ	しょ	しょ	しょ	しょ

JA

じゃ	じゃ	じゃ	じゃ	じゃ	じゃ

First, **TRACE** each character several times, paying strict attention to stroke order and direction. Then carefully draw the character in the blank squares. Take your time. Develop good habits NOW.

JU

じゅ	じゅ	じゅ	じゅ	じゅ	じゅ

JO

じょ	じょ	じょ	じょ	じょ	じょ

CHA

ちゃ	ちゃ	ちゃ	ちゃ	ちゃ	ちゃ

CHU

ちゅ	ちゅ	ちゅ	ちゅ	ちゅ	ちゅ

CHO

ちょ	ちょ	ちょ	ちょ	ちょ	ちょ

JA

ぢゃ	ぢゃ	ぢゃ	ぢゃ	ぢゃ	ぢゃ

First, **TRACE** each character several times, paying strict attention to stroke order and direction. Then carefully draw the character in the blank squares. Take your time. Develop good habits NOW.

JU

ぢゅ	ぢゅ	ぢゅ	ぢゅ	ぢゅ	ぢゅ

JO

ぢょ	ぢょ	ぢょ	ぢょ	ぢょ	ぢょ

NYA

にゃ	にゃ	にゃ	にゃ	にゃ	にゃ

NYU

にゅ	にゅ	にゅ	にゅ	にゅ	にゅ

NYO

にょ	にょ	にょ	にょ	にょ	にょ

HYA

ひゃ	ひゃ	ひゃ	ひゃ	ひゃ	ひゃ

First, **TRACE** each character several times, paying strict attention to stroke order and direction. Then carefully draw the character in the blank squares. Take your time. Develop good habits NOW.

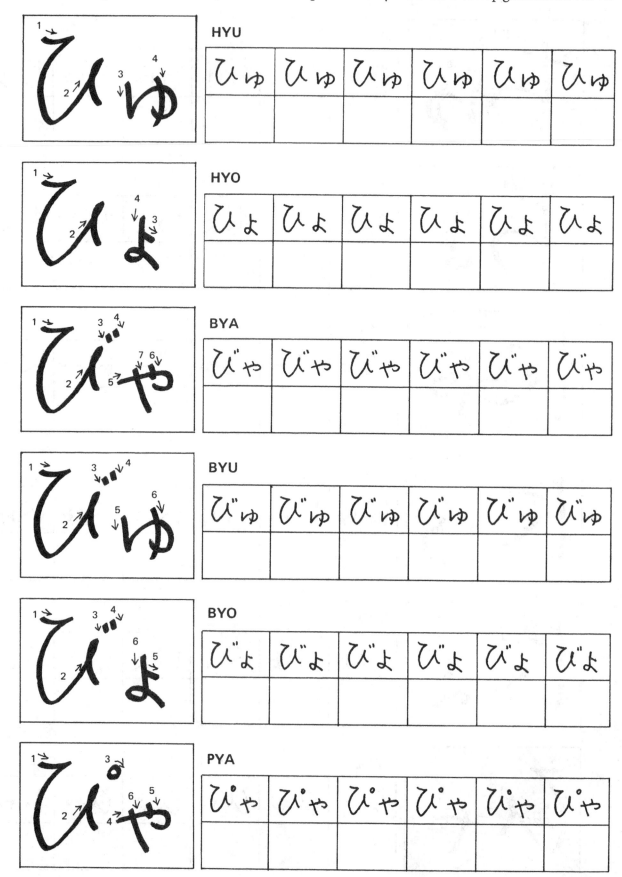

HYU

ひゅ ひゅ ひゅ ひゅ ひゅ ひゅ

HYO

ひょ ひょ ひょ ひょ ひょ ひょ

BYA

びゃ びゃ びゃ びゃ びゃ びゃ

BYU

びゅ びゅ びゅ びゅ びゅ びゅ

BYO

びょ びょ びょ びょ びょ びょ

PYA

ぴゃ ぴゃ ぴゃ ぴゃ ぴゃ ぴゃ

First, **TRACE** each character several times, paying strict attention to stroke order and direction. Then carefully draw the character in the blank squares. Take your time. Develop good habits NOW.

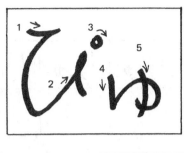

PYU

ぴゅ	ぴゅ	ぴゅ	ぴゅ	ぴゅ	ぴゅ

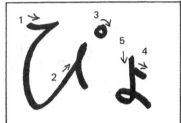

PYO

ぴょ	ぴょ	ぴょ	ぴょ	ぴょ	ぴょ

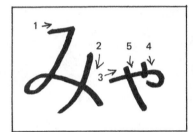

MYA

みゃ	みゃ	みゃ	みゃ	みゃ	みゃ

MYU

みゅ	みゅ	みゅ	みゅ	みゅ	みゅ

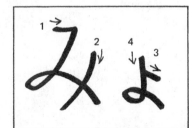

MYO

みょ	みょ	みょ	みょ	みょ	みょ

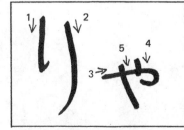

RYA

りゃ	りゃ	りゃ	りゃ	りゃ	りゃ

First, **TRACE** each character several times, paying strict attention to stroke order and direction. Then carefully draw the character in the blank squares. Take your time. Develop good habits NOW.

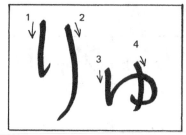

RYU

りゅ	りゅ	りゅ	りゅ	りゅ	りゅ

RYO

りょ	りょ	りょ	りょ	りょ	りょ

Writing words in Hiragana

This section will teach you how double consonants and long vowels are made, and give you some practice at writing words.

Double consonants

There are certain consonant sounds in the Japanese sound system that may be doubled, specifically /K/, /S/ (including /SH/), /T/ (including /CH/), and /P/. Note that only voiceless consonants may be doubled.

In each case the double consonant is represented in *HIRAGANA* by a small *TSU* (つ) placed immediately BEFORE the consonant sound to be doubled, as in the examples below.

Notice that the *TSU* (つ) character is smaller than it would normally be written. Compare the following pairs:

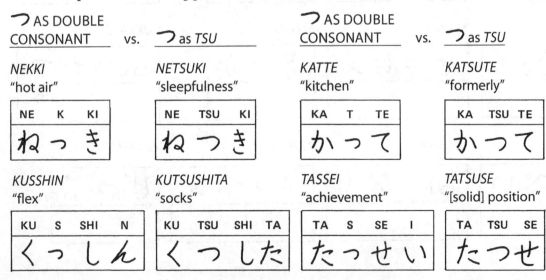

Practice writing the following words that have double consonants. First, **TRACE** the *HIRAGANA* characters as shown, being careful to follow correct stroke order and direction as learned previously. Then write the words, character for character, in the blank spaces. These words were selected for writing practice only. We advise that you NOT waste time looking up their meanings.

ASSARI
あっさり

BASSAI
ばっさい

HASSEN
はっせん

ISSOKU
いっそく

HASSHA
はっしゃ

JISSHIN
じっしん

OSSHARU
おっしゃる

ZASSHI
ざっし

TOTTSUKI
とっつき

MITTSU
みっつ

OTTSUKE
おっつけ

SHITTSUI
しっつい

TATTOBU
たっとぶ

ZETTAI
ぜったい

KUTTAKU
くったく

MUTTO
むっと

ETCHAN
えっちゃん

KITCHIRI
きっちり

SATCHI
さっち

SOTCHOKU
そっちょく

KEKKYOKU
けっきょく

SEKKEN
せっけん

MAKKA
まっか

FUKKATSU
ふっかつ

EPPEI
えっぺい

CHOPPIRI
ちょっぴり

TEPPEN
てっぺん

GEPPU
げっぷ

NOTE: Don't be confused when you see words that are romanized with double *N*, such as *ZANNEN*, *KONNICHI*, *MINNA*, etc. These are not treated as double consonants in *HIRAGANA*, since the first *N* is represented by the character ん, as follows:

ZANNEN

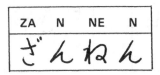

KONNICHI

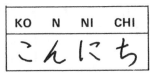

MINNA

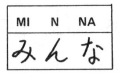

The character for *TSU* (っ) is NEVER used to double the consonant *N*.

Long vowels

Long vowels are usually represented in *RŌMAJI* by a vowel with a line over it, as in *OKĀSAN*, *SENSHŪ*, *ONĒSAN*, *ŌSAKA*. The vowel *I* (and in some other forms of romanization, *A*, *O*, *E*, and *U* as well) may be romanized by repeating the vowel, as in *ONIISAN* and *CHIISAI*.

In *HIRAGANA* long vowels are usually represented by placing あ *(A)*, い *(I)*, う *(U)*, え *(E)*, or お *(O)* immediately after the character that has the corresponding vowel sound. In other words, as follows:

OKĀSAN

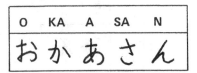

ONIISAN

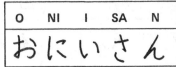

SENSHŪ

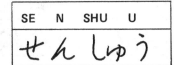

ONĒSAN

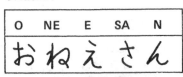

ŌSAKA

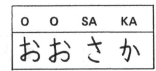

The exception to this rule is that the vowel *O* is often elongated by use of the character う *(U)*, instead of お *(O)*. Ordinarily, お is used to elongate an *O* that BEGINS a word, as in *ŌSAKA* (お おさか) and *ŌKII* (お おきい). When the long *O* is in the MIDDLE of a word or at the END of a word, the character う is more often used, as in

GAKKŌ

GA	K	KO	U

がっこう

RYŌSHIN

RYO	U	SHI	N

りょうしん

Rare exceptions to this rule should be memorized as you come across them. (Appendix B includes a brief list of common exceptions.)

Now practice writing the following words that have long vowels. First, **TRACE** the *HIRAGANA*, then write each word, character for character, in the space provided. Always be careful to follow the appropriate stroke order as learned previously.

BĀYA
ばあや

OKĀSAN
おかあさん

MĀ
まあ

OGYĀ
おぎゃあ

ATARASHII
あたらしい

OJIISAN
おじいさん

CHII
ちい

IIE
いいえ

KŪKI
くうき

RAISHŪ
らいしゅう

TSŪSHIN
つうしん

SEIYŪ
せいゆう

Ē
ええ

ONĒSAN
おねえさん

ĒTO
ええと

HĒ
へえ

ŌKII
おおきい

ŌSAKA
おおさか

ŌJO
おおじょ

ŌI
おおい

RYOKŌ
りょこう

SHŌKAI
しょうかい

SHACHŌ
しゃちょう

HIKŌKI
ひこうき

OBĀSAN
おばあさん

ONIISAN
おにいさん

FŪTŌ
ふうとう

SŪ
すう

Writing sentences in Hiragana

Particles

Other than the rules and guidelines given heretofore, there are few things to remember when writing sentences in *KANA*. There are, however, a couple of exceptions in the writing of particles.

A. The topic particle *WA* is written NOT with the character わ , but with the character は *(HA)*. This is the ONLY time that は is not pronounced HA, and it is the ONLY time that the syllable *WA* is not written with わ. Note that the *WA* in *DEWA MATA, DEWA ARIMASEN,* and *DEWA ARI-MASEN DESHITA* is related to the particle *WA* and is included in this rule.

Practice writing the following short sentences by first tracing the characters as given, then writing them in the spaces provided.

KORE WA HON DEWA ARIMASEN.

これ は ほん では ありません。

KARE WA GAKUSEI DEWA ARIMASEN DESHITA.

かれ は がくせい では ありません でした。

continued

B. The direction particle *E* is written NOT with the character え, but with the character へ (*HE*). This is the ONLY time that へ is not pronounced HE, and it is the ONLY time that the syllable *E* is not written with the character え.

Practice writing the following short sentences by first tracing the characters as given, then writing the characters in the spaces provided.

WATAKUSHI WA HON'YA E IKIMASU.

わたくし は ほんや へ いきます。

KANOJO WA YŪBINKYOKU E IKIMASHITA.

かのじょ は ゆうびんきょく へ いきました。

C. The direct object particle *O* is written with the character を. This is the only use for the character を. Any other time that the syllable *O* occurs (as in *ONAMAE, EGAO, KIOKU,* etc.), it is written with the character お.

Practice writing the following short sentences by first tracing the characters as given, then writing the characters in the spaces provided.

TOSHIO-SAN WA HON O KAIMASHITA.

としおさん は ほん を かいました。

OTŌSAN WA ŌKII KURUMA O MOTTE IMASU.

おとうさん は おおきい くるま を もって います。

Spaces

In ordinary Japanese reading material, when both *KANA* and *KANJI* are used, there are few—if any—spaces placed between words. However, when KANA is used exclusively, or when few *KANJI* are used, spaces are provided to make it easier to read and understand the meaning.

Notice the visual differences in the two versions of the following sentence:

WATAKUSHI WA YŪSHOKU O TABETE, HEYA NI ITTE, TEGAMI O KAKIMASHITA.

a) わたくし は ゆうしょく を たべて、 へや に
いって、 てがみ を かきました。

b) 私 は 夕食 を 食べて、 部屋 に 行って、 手紙 を 書
きました。

In version a), if there were no spaces to separate the words, it would be difficult to understand. In version b), however, the function of the spaces is performed by the *KANJI* characters, and so no spaces are really needed.

You should be aware that the Japanese often omit the space between a word and the particle that follows it, as well as spaces between the words of a verb phrase, as in the following example:

WATAKUSHI WA YŪSHOKU O TABETE, O-MISE NI ITTE KIMASHITA.

わたくしは ゆうしょくを たべて、 おみせに
いってきました。

Punctuation and miscellany

There are few rules of punctuation in Japanese, and there is a great deal of flexibility in their use. The major marks of punctuation are as follows:

A. ☐ ○ *KUTEN* (period; also called *MARU*, meaning "circle")

This is used, as in English, to mark the end of a sentence. It also may mark the end of a question or an exclamatory sentence, after particles *KA* and *YO*. In casual writing, it has become common for the English question mark (?) and exclamation point (!) to be used instead, but it is still most common for the *KUTEN* to be used alone after the particle.

B. ☐ 、 *TŌTEN* (comma; literally, "reading point")

Rules for the use of *TŌTEN* are much less rigid than English rules for using commas, to the point that their use is almost arbitrary. They may be placed wherever a natural break in the sentence would occur—always AFTER a particle or conjunction, rather than before one.

continued

C. 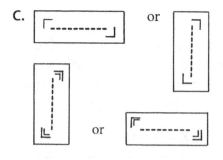 or

KAKKO or *KAGIKAKKO* (quotation marks)

Used much as in English, these are placed to the upper left and lower right of the first and last characters, respectively, of the word or words quoted in horizontal writing, but to the upper right and lower left of words quoted in vertical writing. (See examples in the practice and self-test section, starting on page 39.) It is also possible to make double quotations, as shown at left, although these are rarely used in Japanese.

D. OTHER MARKS

The Japanese find use for brackets [ ] , 〈 〉 and parentheses ( ) in situations similar to those for which they would be used in English. There is no strictly Japanese counterpart for these in current use. All are referred to as *KAKKO*.

Although hyphens (-) may be used when writing in *RŌMAJI*, they are never used when writing in Japanese script. However, occasionally a dash (—) may be used to indicate an interruption in thought, a long pause, or in place of a colon. Colons and semicolons are not used with Japanese script.

Underlining, paragraphs, and line breaks

To place visual emphasis on or call attention to a word or words, the Japanese may underline them as in English, except that in vertical writing the line is drawn to the right of the characters. (See examples under "Vertical writing," on the next page.)

Paragraphs are indicated by an indentation, as in English. The indentation for Japanese script is usually the size of one character. Since Japanese characters represent syllables, the breaking of a word (at the end of a line, for example) may be done between any two characters, even between the two elements of a combination character. Lines may, therefore, be kept fairly uniform in length. There are no hyphens to indicate when a word has been broken at the end of a line, just as there may be no spaces between words. Once you become accustomed to reading without these English-style cues, they are not particularly missed.

Vertical writing

Shown below are two samples of *HIRAGANA* written vertically, one in machine-made characters and the other handwritten. Take careful note of the spacing and positioning of the characters, particularly the double consonant symbols (*) and combination characters (lined). Also notice how the quotation marks and other punctuation are arranged.

ひなたちは かえってきた ひばりに いいました。
「おかあさん。 たいへん です。 あした おひゃくしょうさんが、むぎかりに くるそうですよ。」
ひばりは こたえました。
「だいじょうぶですよ。 けっして しんぱい いりません。」

Kana repetition symbols

You should be aware of two symbols of repetition that are used by the Japanese, particularly in vertical writing. The first (example A, below) repeats only one *KANA* character; the second (example B) is used to repeat two or more characters. Symbol B is used ONLY in vertical writing. In words where a voiceless character or characters is repeated VOICED, the usual *NIGORI* symbol is used with the repetition symbol.

These symbols are not as commonly used today as formerly, but you will still see them from time to time as you practice reading Japanese.

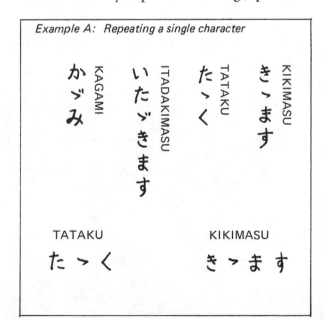

Example A: Repeating a single character

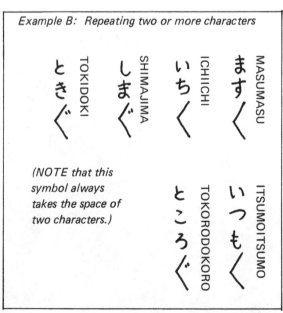

Example B: Repeating two or more characters

(NOTE that this symbol always takes the space of two characters.)

Hiragana practice
and self-test

On the following pages are exercises to help you practice reading and writing in *HIRAGANA*.

Follow the instructions carefully. Some of the exercises require that you TRACE, COPY, and then ROMANIZE sentences given for you in *HIRAGANA*. Other exercises require that you write in *HIRAGANA* sentences that are presented in *RŌMAJI*.

In some exercises the *HIRAGANA* is presented in machine-made characters; in others it is handwritten. Some exercises are written horizontally; some are written vertically. Every effort has been made to give you experience in a variety of writing situations, as well as to expose you to some slightly different handwriting styles.

After you have finished each exercise, check your work carefully against the correct responses given in Appendix C in the back of this book. Translations of the sentences used in this section are given in Appendix D.

First, TRACE the following sentences, then COPY them, character for character, in the first blank space for each line. In the second blank space, ROMANIZE what you have written.

1) これ は なん です か。 2) それ は とけい

です。 3) あの ひと は だれ です か。 4) か

のじょ は たなかさん です。 5) しょくどう は あ

そこ です か。 6) おてあらい は どこ です か。

7) かれ は せんせい ではありません。 8) あの

ひと は がいじん です か。 9) ゆうびんきょく

は むこう です。 10) わたくし は がくせい

でした。 11) いりぐち は あそこ です ね。

Check your work against correct responses given in Appendix C.

First, TRACE the following sentences, then COPY them, character for character, in the first blank space for each line. In the second blank space, ROMANIZE what you have written.

りなん です か。 ²としょかん は どこ に

ありますか。 ³ぎんこう は むこう に

あります。 ⁴じゅうぎょういん は どこ に い

ます か。 ⁵じゅうぎょういん は あの へや

に います。 ⁶あの へや に は ごみ ば

こ が あります か。 ⁷きょうしつ に つく

え が ありません。 ⁸あの へや に だ

れ が いました か。 ⁹かれ は いません。

First, TRACE the following sentences, then COPY them, character for character, in the first blank space for each line. In the second blank space, ROMANIZE what you have written.

<table>
<tr><td>trace</td><td>りよく　いらっしゃいました。²どこ　へ　いきま</td></tr>
<tr><td>copy</td><td></td></tr>
<tr><td>rōmaji</td><td></td></tr>
</table>

<table>
<tr><td>trace</td><td>す　か。³けさ　がっこう　に　きました。⁴き</td></tr>
<tr><td>copy</td><td></td></tr>
<tr><td>rōmaji</td><td></td></tr>
</table>

<table>
<tr><td>trace</td><td>のう　たなかさん　は　じむしょ　に　きません　で</td></tr>
<tr><td>copy</td><td></td></tr>
<tr><td>rōmaji</td><td></td></tr>
</table>

<table>
<tr><td>trace</td><td>した。⁵しゃちょうさん　は　きょう　たくしい　で　かえ</td></tr>
<tr><td>copy</td><td></td></tr>
<tr><td>rōmaji</td><td></td></tr>
</table>

<table>
<tr><td>trace</td><td>りました。⁶あなた　は　もう　かえります　か。</td></tr>
<tr><td>copy</td><td></td></tr>
<tr><td>rōmaji</td><td></td></tr>
</table>

<table>
<tr><td>trace</td><td>⁷かのじょ　は　なんで　とうきょう　に　いきました</td></tr>
<tr><td>copy</td><td></td></tr>
<tr><td>rōmaji</td><td></td></tr>
</table>

<table>
<tr><td>trace</td><td>か。⁸わたくし　は　きのう　ゆうびんきょく　へ</td></tr>
<tr><td>copy</td><td></td></tr>
<tr><td>rōmaji</td><td></td></tr>
</table>

<table>
<tr><td>trace</td><td>いきません　でした。⁹かれ　は　ともだち　です。</td></tr>
<tr><td>copy</td><td></td></tr>
<tr><td>rōmaji</td><td></td></tr>
</table>

Check your work against correct responses given in Appendix C.

First, TRACE the following sentences, then COPY them, character for character, in the first blank space for each line. In the second blank space, ROMANIZE what you have written.

trace	あの　ひと　は　にほんご　を　べんきょう　して
copy	
rōmaji	

trace	います　か。　しゃちょうさん　に　もう　いちど
copy	
rōmaji	

trace	でんわ　を　して　ください。　かのじょ　は　しん
copy	
rōmaji	

trace	ぶん　を　よんで　いません。　たなかさん　は
copy	
rōmaji	

trace	くるま　を　ゆうびんきょく　まで　うんてん　しま
copy	
rōmaji	

trace	した。　わたくし　は　ほんや　へ　いきました
copy	
rōmaji	

trace	けれども、　ほん　を　かいません　でした。　きょ
copy	
rōmaji	

trace	う　わたくし　と　たべて　くださいません　か。
copy	
rōmaji	

Check your work against correct responses given in Appendix C.

Hiragana practice and self-test　43

First, TRACE the following sentences, then COPY them, character for character, in the first blank space for each line. In the second blank space, ROMANIZE what you have written.

あなた は なぜ きょうしつ に いきません

か。 あした まで でんわ しないで ください。

らいしゅう また くる こと が できます か。

こんばん いそがしい です から、いく こと

が できません。 おきゃくさま が すぐ きます

ので、まだ かえらないで ください。 おにい

さん は なぜ たべません でした か。 じゅ

いちじ まで べんきょう しましょう、ね。

First, TRACE the following sentences, then COPY them, character for character, in the blank space to the right of each line. Then ROMANIZE them on the blank horizontal lines at the bottom.

| trace | copy | trace | copy | trace | copy | trace | copy | trace | copy | trace | copy | trace | copy | trace | copy |

1.
どう いう いみ です か。
2. しつもん が あります か。

3. おはよう ございます。
4. おやすみ なさい。
5. ああ、そ

う です か。
6. では また。
7. わかります、でしょう。

8. さようなら。
9. いくら です か。
10. いちまんごせん にひ

やくじゅうどる です。
11. たかい です、ね。
12. いいえ、

やすい です よ。
13. おなまえ は なん です か。
14. た

なか と もうします。
15. はじめまして。
16. よろしく お

ねがい します。
17. どうも ありがとう ございます。
18. どう

いたしまして。
19. きゅうひゃくろくじゅうごえん です。

Romanize:

First, TRACE the following sentences, then COPY them, character for character, in the blank space to the right of each line. Then ROMANIZE them on the blank horizontal lines at the bottom.

trace	copy	trace	copy	trace	copy	trace	copy	trace	copy	trace	copy	trace	copy	trace	copy

1.
でぐち は どこ です か。 2. いりぐち は むこう です、

ね。 3. かれ は せんせい では ありません か。 4. わたく

し の だいがく は とうきょう に あります。 5. あなた

の つくえ は どれ です か。 6. ざんねん です、ね。

7. じむしょ に は ごみばこ も とけい も あります。

8. どの へや が かれ の です か。 9. きょうしつ に は、

せんせい も がくせい も います。 10. しゃちょうさん と

じゅうぎょういん は いま その へや に います か。

11. あなた の くるま は むこう に ありません でした。

Romanize:

_____

_____

_____

_____

_____

_____

_____

_____

Check your work against the correct responses in Appendix C.

First, TRACE the following sentences, then COPY them, character for character, in the blank space to the right of each line. Then ROMANIZE them on the blank horizontal lines at the bottom.

1.

trace	copy	trace	copy	trace	copy	trace	copy	trace	copy	trace	copy	trace	copy	trace	copy

と は いま へや で てがみ を よんで います。

た。 11. おとうと は おおさか で はたらいて います か。 12. いもう

10. さくばん だいがく の でぐち で たなかさん と まって いまし

した。 9. かれ は じゅうじ じゅうごふん まえ に かえりました。

あさん と おねえさん は いっしょ に しょくどう で たべて いま

ま でした。 6. ちょっと まって ください。 7. いって きます。 8. おか

おねえさん と いっしょ に ちかてつ で かえります。 5. ごちそうさ

しゅう ゆうびんきょく へ いきました か。 4. らいしゅう まいにち

いらっしゃいませ。 2. こんど は いっしょ に いきましょう。 3. せん

Romanize: _____

_____

_____

_____

_____

_____

_____

_____

Check your work against the correct responses in Appendix C.

Hiragana practice and self-test 47

First, TRACE the following sentences, then COPY them, character for character, in the blank space to the right of each line. Then ROMANIZE them on the blank horizontal lines at the bottom.

trace	copy	trace	copy	trace	copy	trace	copy	trace	copy	trace	copy	trace	copy	trace	copy	trace	copy
から、わたくしたち は しごと へ いきません。		まだ しょくじ が できません。 10. げつようび は きゅうじつ です		して ください ません か。 9. おなか が すいて います けれども、		して います。 8. あした の あさ、がっこう で せんせい と はな		できます か。 7. おとうさん は ことし にほん で りょこう を		で まだ ほん を かわないで ください。 6. みんな は にほんご が		う する こと が できません でした。 5. おかね が ありません の		も どこ で きゅうけい を します か。 4. いちにちぢゅう べんきょ		おじゃま します。 2. おたんじょうび おめでとう ございます。 3. いつ	

Romanize:

_____

_____

_____

_____

_____

_____

_____

_____

Check your work against the correct responses in Appendix C.

First, COPY each line of the dialogue below onto the first blank space beneath it. In the second blank space ROMANIZE each line of dialogue. Check your work carefully against Appendix C.

たなか 「せんせい は きょうしつ に います か。」

romaji / _copy_

ほんだ 「いいえ、 じむしょ に います。」

romaji / _copy_

たなか 「じむしょ は どこ に あります か。」

romaji / _copy_

ほんだ 「むこう に あります。」

romaji / _copy_

たなか 「この へん に は ごみばこ が あります か。」

romaji / _copy_

ほんだ 「ごみばこ は あの へや に あります。」

romaji / _copy_

たなか 「おてあらい も あります か。」

romaji / _copy_

ほんだ 「いいえ、 ありません。 としょかん に あります。」

romaji / _copy_

たなか 「どうも ありがとう ございます。」

romaji / _copy_

First, COPY each line of the dialogue below onto the blank space to the right of it. Then write the dialogue in *ROMAJI* on the lines at the bottom of the page. Check your work against Appendix C.

あき　「はい、あした は けっこう です よ。」

さとう　「いい です よ。あした は どう です か。」

できません。ごめん なさい、ね。

あき　「すみません が、きょう いそいで います ので、

いきましょう か。」

さとう　「はい、わかりました。では、としょかん へ

あき　「きょう いません から、まだ しないで ください。」

さとう　「おともだち に でんわ を しましょう か。」

Romanize:

_____

_____

_____

_____

_____

_____

_____

Write the following sentences in *HIRAGANA* in the spaces provided. Check your work carefully against the correct responses given in Appendix C.

1. *SORE WA ANATA NO HON DESU KA?*

2. *KARE WA SENSEI DEWA ARIMASEN DESHITA.*

3. *TOSHOKAN WA MUKŌ DESU.*

4. *ANATA WA GAKUSEI DEWA ARIMASEN KA?*

5. *YŪBINKYOKU WA DORE DESU KA?*

6. *SORE WA KANOJO NO JISHO DESU, NE?*

7. *ANO HITO NO TSUKUE WA ASOKO DESU.*

8. *TANAKA-SAN NO TOKEI WA TAKAI, DESHŌ?*

9. *ANO HITOBITO WA DAIGAKUSEI DESHITA.*

10. *MUKŌ NO HITO WA SHACHŌ-SAN DESU, NE?*

11. *HON'YA-SAN WA GAIJIN DESU.*

12. *WATAKUSHI-TACHI WA NIHONJIN DEWA ARIMASEN.*

Write the following sentences in *HIRAGANA* in the spaces provided. Check your work carefully against the correct responses given in Appendix C.

1. *O-TOMODACHI WA IMA SHOKUDŌ NI IMASU.*

2. *O-TEARAI WA DOKO NI ARIMASU KA?*

3. *WATAKUSHI WA KURUMA GA ARIMASEN.*

4. *KANOJO WA SENSHŪ TŌKYŌ NI IMASHITA.*

5. *SEITO-TACHI WA KINŌ KYŌSHITSU NI IMASEN DESHITA.*

6. *ANO HEYA NI WA DARE GA IMASU KA?*

7. *KONO JITENSHA WA KARE NO DEWA ARIMASEN.*

8. *JŪGYŌIN MO SHACHŌ-SAN MO JIMUSHO NI IMASU.*

9. *GOMIBAKO MO O-TEARAI NI ARIMASU KA?*

10. *ANO HITOBITO WA KINŌ NO ASA YŪBINKYOKU NI IMASHITA.*

11. *SHOKUDŌ WA ASOKO NI ARIMASU, NE?*

12. *GINKŌ MO TOSHOKAN MO SOKO NI ARIMASU.*

Write the following sentences in *HIRAGANA* in the spaces provided. Check your work carefully against the correct responses given in Appendix C.

1. *ANATA WA KYŌ TOSHOKAN NI IKIMASU KA?*

2. *YŪBE SHOKUDŌ E IKIMASEN DESHITA.*

3. *SHACHŌ-SAN WA HIKŌKI DE TŌKYŌ E IKIMASHITA, DESHŌ?*

4. *ONĒSAN WA MAINICHI CHIKATETSU DE KAERIMASU.*

5. *SENGETSU MINNA WA DENSHA DE KIMASHITA.*

6. *RAINEN FUNE DE IKIMASHŌ.*

7. *ONIISAN TO ISSHO NI KIMASHITA, NE?*

8. *IMA WATAKUSHI WA JIKAN GA ARIMASEN.*

9. *IMŌTO-SAN WA MŌ KAERIMASHITA KA?*

10. *O-TOMODACHI WA HIKŌKI DE CHŪGOKU E KAERIMASHITA KA?*

11. *GO-SHUJIN WA SAKUBAN NO KAI NI IKIMASHITA KA?*

12. *TANAKA-SAN WA ASHITA SAPPORO E KAERIMASU.*

Write the following sentences in *HIRAGANA* in the spaces provided. Check your work carefully against the correct responses given in Appendix C.

1. *ANATA WA IMA NANI O SHITE IMASU KA?*

2. *KARE NO RYŌSHIN WA ŌSAKA NI SUNDE IMASU.*

3. *KANOJO WA HEYA DE TEGAMI O KAITE IMASU.*

4. *ONIISAN TO OTŌSAN WA ISSHO NI HASHITTE IMASHITA.*

5. *O-TOMODACHI TO MUKŌ NI SUWATTE KUDASAI.*

6. *MINNA WA MŌ UCHI E KAETTE IMASU.*

7. *SUKOSHI BENKYŌ SHITE KUDASAIMASEN KA?*

8. *TOSHOKAN E IKIMASU KEREDOMO, BENKYŌ SHIMASEN.*

9. *TANAKA-SAN WA KESA MUKŌ NI TATTE IMASHITA.*

10. *KANOJO-TACHI WA MADA KYŪKEI O SHITE IMASU.*

11. *ANO UTA O UTATTE KUDASAIMASU KA?*

12. *WATAKUSHI WA GINKŌ DE HATARAITE IMASEN DESHITA.*

Write the following sentences in *HIRAGANA* in the spaces provided. Check your work carefully against the correct responses given in Appendix C.

1. *ASHITA WA KYŪJITSU DESU KARA, YASUNDE KUDASAI.*

2. *NIHONGO O HANASU KOTO GA DEKIMASU KA?*

3. *BYŌKI DESU NODE, JIMUSHO E IKANAIDE KUDASAI.*

4. *RAIGETSU NO KAI NI IKU KOTO GA DEKIMASEN KA?*

5. *KANOJO WA UTAU KOTO GA DEKIMASEN.*

6. *MŌ SUKOSHI MATSU KOTO GA DEKIMASU KA?*

7. *TAKAI DESU NODE, KAWANAIDE KUDASAI.*

8. *ANATA WA NAZE HANKAGAI E IKIMASEN DESHITA KA?*

9. *JIKAN GA ARIMASEN KARA, MADA TABENAIDE KUDASAI.*

10. *KYŌSHITSU DE TOMODACHI TO HANASANAIDE KUDASAI.*

11. *KURUMA GA ARIMASEN KARA, DENSHA DE IKIMASU.*

12. *EIGO GA DEKIMASEN NODE, NIHONGO DE HANASHITE IMASHITA.*

PART TWO

Katakana no gojūon

The 50 sounds of Katakana

The chart below contains the "50 sounds" (again, actually only 46 symbols) of the *KATAKANA* syllabary.

Note that these characters represent the same sounds as *HIRAGANA*; only the usage is different. *KATAKANA* is used primarily to write words and names of foreign origin. It is also used to place emphasis on or call attention to a word or phrase and is used liberally in advertising.

Begin here. ↓

ワ WA	ラ RA	ヤ YA	マ MA	ハ HA	ナ NA	タ TA	サ SA	カ KA	ア A
	リ RI		ミ MI	ヒ HI	ニ NI	チ CHI	シ SHI	キ KI	イ I
	ル RU	ユ YU	ム MU	フ FU	ヌ NU	ツ TSU	ス SU	ク KU	ウ U
	レ RE		メ ME	ヘ HE	ネ NE	テ TE	セ SE	ケ KE	エ E
ヲ (W)O	ロ RO	ヨ YO	モ MO	ホ HO	ノ NO	ト TO	ソ SO	コ KO	オ O
ン N'									

This chart is given in machine-made characters in Appendix A.

Writing Katakana characters

Review the information on page 5 about writing *KANA*, then proceed with the *KATAKANA* writing exercises that begin on the next page. As always, be careful to follow correct stroke order and stroke direction, as indicated by the numbers and arrows accompanying each demonstration character. Take your time. Use this opportunity to develop good writing habits and penmanship.

First, **TRACE** each character several times, paying strict attention to stroke order and direction. Then carefully draw the character in the blank squares. Take your time. Develop good habits NOW.

A

ア	ア	ア	ア	ア	ア	ア	ア	ア

I

イ	イ	イ	イ	イ	イ	イ	イ	イ

U

ウ	ウ	ウ	ウ	ウ	ウ	ウ	ウ	ウ

E

エ	エ	エ	エ	エ	エ	エ	エ	エ

O

オ	オ	オ	オ	オ	オ	オ	オ	オ

KA

カ	カ	カ	カ	カ	カ	カ	カ	カ

First, **TRACE** each character several times, paying strict attention to stroke order and direction. Then carefully draw the character in the blank squares. Take your time. Develop good habits NOW.

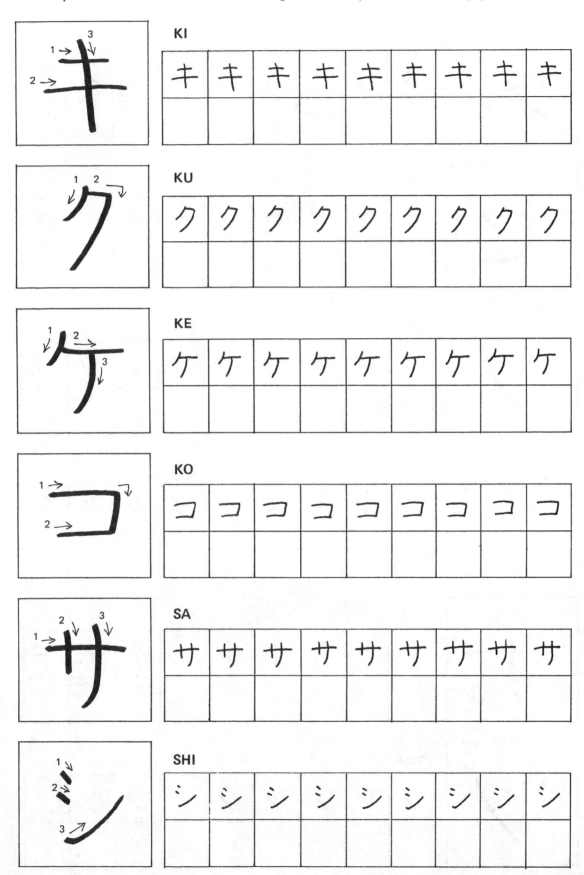

KI

KU

KE

KO

SA

SHI

First, **TRACE** each character several times, paying strict attention to stroke order and direction. Then carefully draw the character in the blank squares. Take your time. Develop good habits NOW.

SU

ス	ス	ス	ス	ス	ス	ス	ス	ス

SE

セ	セ	セ	セ	セ	セ	セ	セ	セ

SO

ソ	ソ	ソ	ソ	ソ	ソ	ソ	ソ	ソ

TA

タ	タ	タ	タ	タ	タ	タ	タ	タ

CHI

チ	チ	チ	チ	チ	チ	チ	チ	チ

TSU

ツ	ツ	ツ	ツ	ツ	ツ	ツ	ツ	ツ

First, **TRACE** each character several times, paying strict attention to stroke order and direction. Then carefully draw the character in the blank squares. Take your time. Develop good habits NOW.

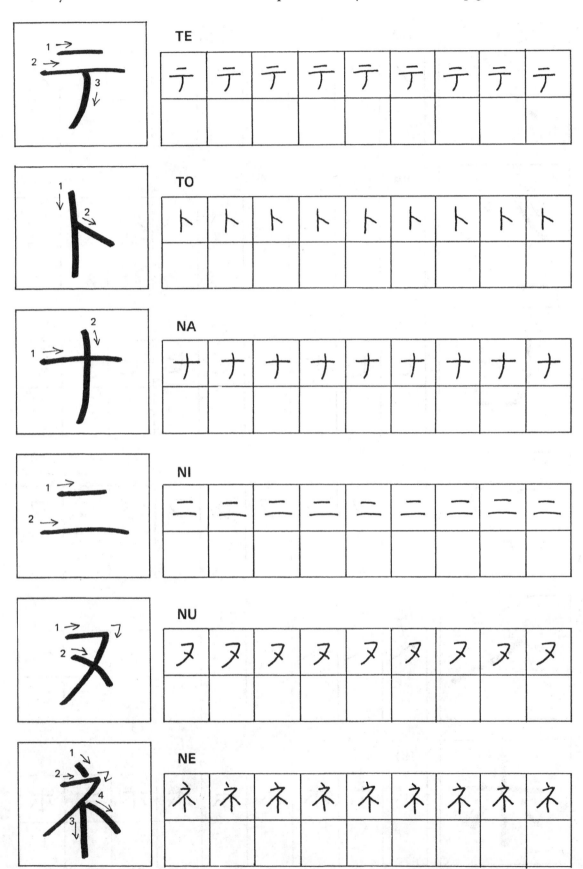

TE

テ テ テ テ テ テ テ テ テ

TO

ト ト ト ト ト ト ト ト ト

NA

ナ ナ ナ ナ ナ ナ ナ ナ ナ

NI

ニ ニ ニ ニ ニ ニ ニ ニ ニ

NU

ヌ ヌ ヌ ヌ ヌ ヌ ヌ ヌ ヌ

NE

ネ ネ ネ ネ ネ ネ ネ ネ ネ

First, **TRACE** each character several times, paying strict attention to stroke order and direction. Then carefully draw the character in the blank squares. Take your time. Develop good habits NOW.

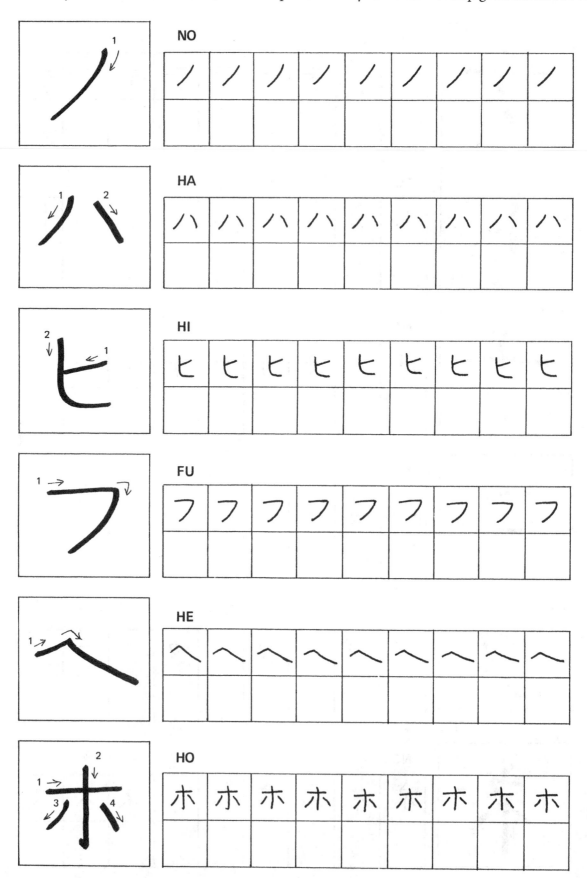

NO

HA

HI

FU

HE

HO

First, **TRACE** each character several times, paying strict attention to stroke order and direction. Then carefully draw the character in the blank squares. Take your time. Develop good habits NOW.

MA

マ マ マ マ マ マ マ マ マ

MI

ミ ミ ミ ミ ミ ミ ミ ミ ミ

MU

ム ム ム ム ム ム ム ム ム

ME

メ メ メ メ メ メ メ メ メ

MO

モ モ モ モ モ モ モ モ モ

YA

ヤ ヤ ヤ ヤ ヤ ヤ ヤ ヤ ヤ

First, **TRACE** each character several times, paying strict attention to stroke order and direction. Then carefully draw the character in the blank squares. Take your time. Develop good habits NOW.

YU

ユ ユ ユ ユ ユ ユ ユ ユ ユ

YO

ヨ ヨ ヨ ヨ ヨ ヨ ヨ ヨ ヨ

RA

ラ ラ ラ ラ ラ ラ ラ ラ ラ

RI

リ リ リ リ リ リ リ リ リ

RU

ル ル ル ル ル ル ル ル ル

RE

レ レ レ レ レ レ レ レ レ

First, **TRACE** each character several times, paying strict attention to stroke order and direction. Then carefully draw the character in the blank squares. Take your time. Develop good habits NOW.

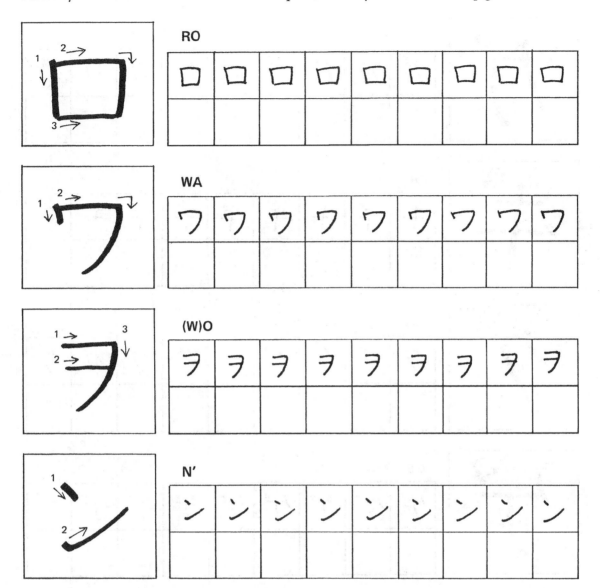

Voiced and voiceless consonants

Now review the information on pages 15 and 16 regarding VOICED and VOICELESS consonants and BILABIALS. All of the information given regarding *HIRAGANA* on those pages is true also for *KATAKANA*.

After you have reviewed that information, proceed with the exercises that begin on the next page on writing these voiced and voiceless characters in *KATAKANA*. Don't rush. Take this opportunity to develop good writing habits and penmanship. Be careful to follow correct stroke order and stroke direction, as indicated by the numbers and arrows accompanying each demonstration character.

First, **TRACE** each character several times, paying strict attention to stroke order and direction. Then carefully draw the character in the blank squares. Take your time. Develop good habits NOW.

GA

ガ	ガ	ガ	ガ	ガ	ガ	ガ	ガ	ガ

GI

ギ	ギ	ギ	ギ	ギ	ギ	ギ	ギ	ギ

GU

グ	グ	グ	グ	グ	グ	グ	グ	グ

GE

ゲ	ゲ	ゲ	ゲ	ゲ	ゲ	ゲ	ゲ	ゲ

GO

ゴ	ゴ	ゴ	ゴ	ゴ	ゴ	ゴ	ゴ	ゴ

ZA

ザ	ザ	ザ	ザ	ザ	ザ	ザ	ザ	ザ

First, **TRACE** each character several times, paying strict attention to stroke order and direction. Then carefully draw the character in the blank squares. Take your time. Develop good habits NOW.

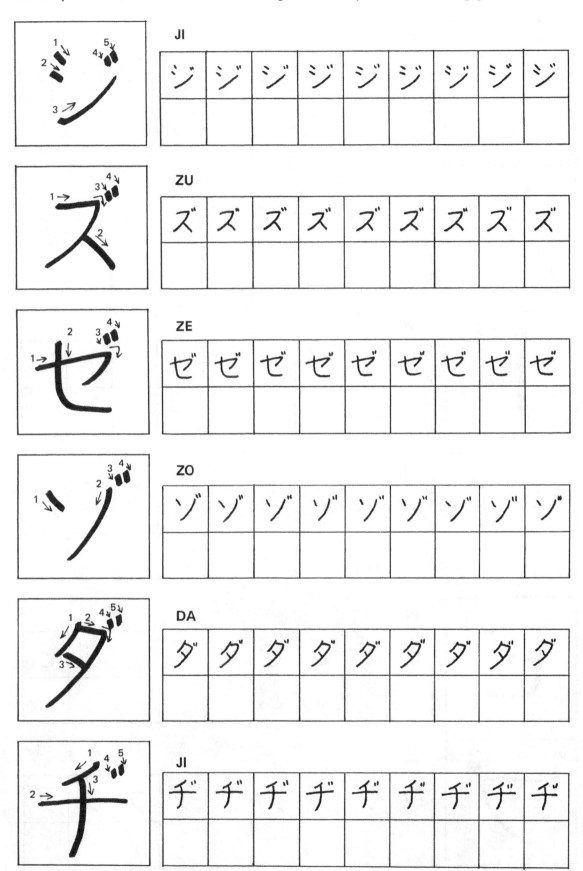

JI

ジ	ジ	ジ	ジ	ジ	ジ	ジ	ジ	ジ

ZU

ズ	ズ	ズ	ズ	ズ	ズ	ズ	ズ	ズ

ZE

ゼ	ゼ	ゼ	ゼ	ゼ	ゼ	ゼ	ゼ	ゼ

ZO

ゾ	ゾ	ゾ	ゾ	ゾ	ゾ	ゾ	ゾ	ゾ

DA

ダ	ダ	ダ	ダ	ダ	ダ	ダ	ダ	ダ

JI

ヂ	ヂ	ヂ	ヂ	ヂ	ヂ	ヂ	ヂ	ヂ

First, **TRACE** each character several times, paying strict attention to stroke order and direction. Then carefully draw the character in the blank squares. Take your time. Develop good habits NOW.

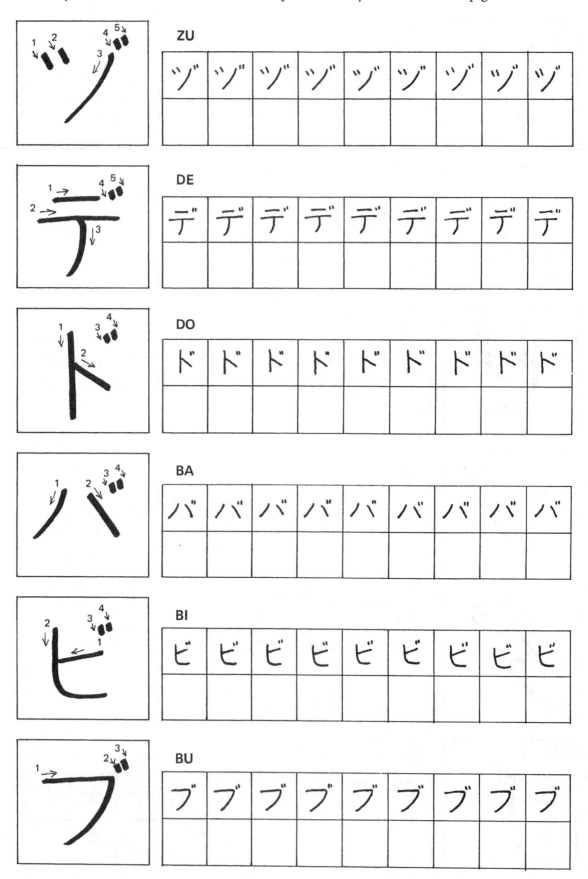

ZU

ヅ ヅ ヅ ヅ ヅ ヅ ヅ ヅ ヅ

DE

デ デ デ デ デ デ デ デ デ

DO

ド ド ド ド ド ド ド ド ド

BA

バ バ バ バ バ バ バ バ バ

BI

ビ ビ ビ ビ ビ ビ ビ ビ ビ

BU

ブ ブ ブ ブ ブ ブ ブ ブ ブ

First, **TRACE** each character several times, paying strict attention to stroke order and direction. Then carefully draw the character in the blank squares. Take your time. Develop good habits NOW.

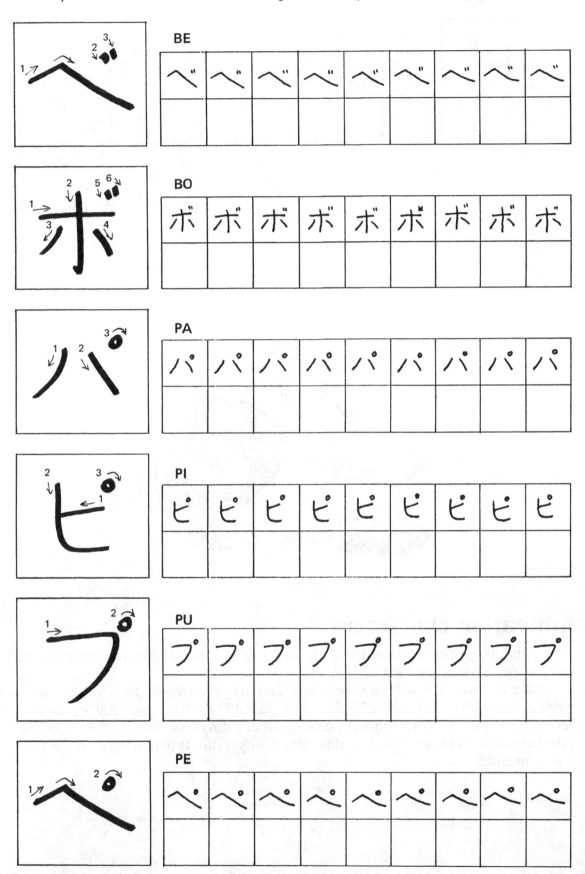

BE

BO

PA

PI

PU

PE

First, **TRACE** each character several times, paying strict attention to stroke order and direction. Then carefully draw the character in the blank squares. Take your time. Develop good habits NOW.

PO								
ポ	ポ	ポ	ポ	ポ	ポ	ポ	ポ	ポ

Combination characters

Review the information on pages 21 and 22. All of the information given regarding *HIRAGANA* on those pages is true also for *KATAKANA*.

After you have reviewed that information carefully, proceed with the following exercises on writing these COMBINATION CHARACTERS in *KATAKANA*. First, TRACE each character several times, paying strict attention to stroke order and direction. Then carefully draw the character in the blank squares. Take your time. Use this opportunity to develop good writing habits and penmanship.

First, **TRACE** each character several times, paying strict attention to stroke order and direction. Then carefully draw the character in the blank squares. Take your time. Develop good habits NOW.

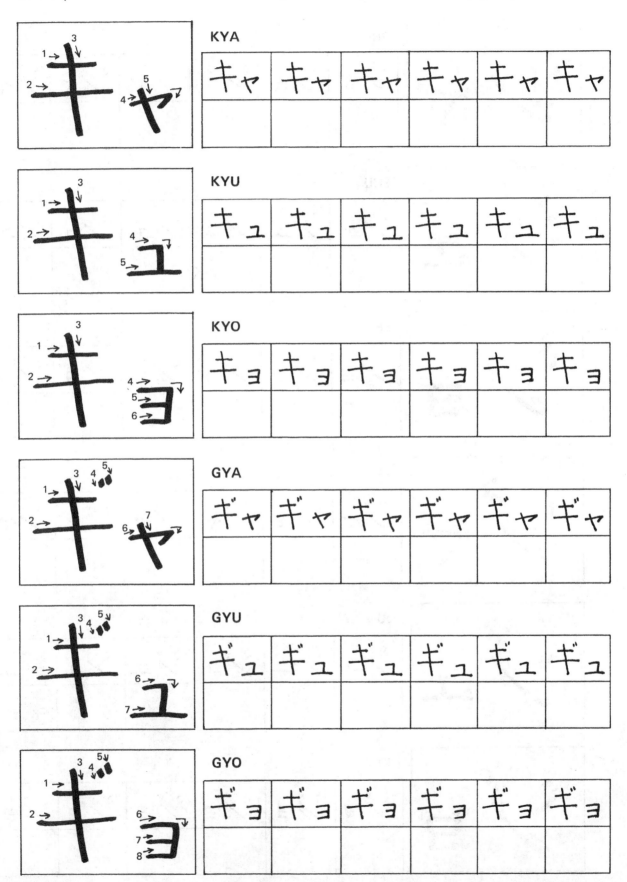

KYA

KYU

KYO

GYA

GYU

GYO

First, **TRACE** each character several times, paying strict attention to stroke order and direction. Then carefully draw the character in the blank squares. Take your time. Develop good habits NOW.

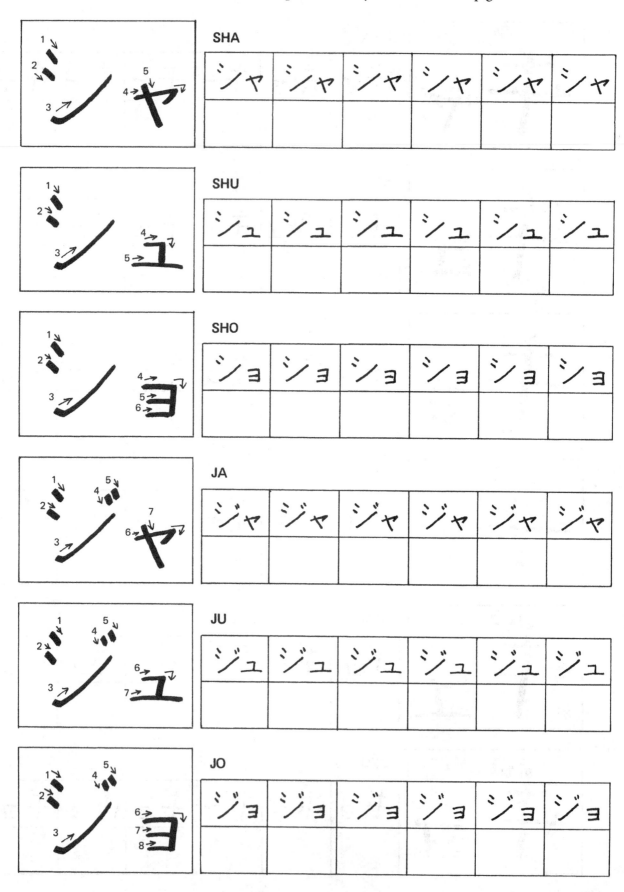

SHA

SHU

SHO

JA

JU

JO

First, **TRACE** each character several times, paying strict attention to stroke order and direction. Then carefully draw the character in the blank squares. Take your time. Develop good habits NOW.

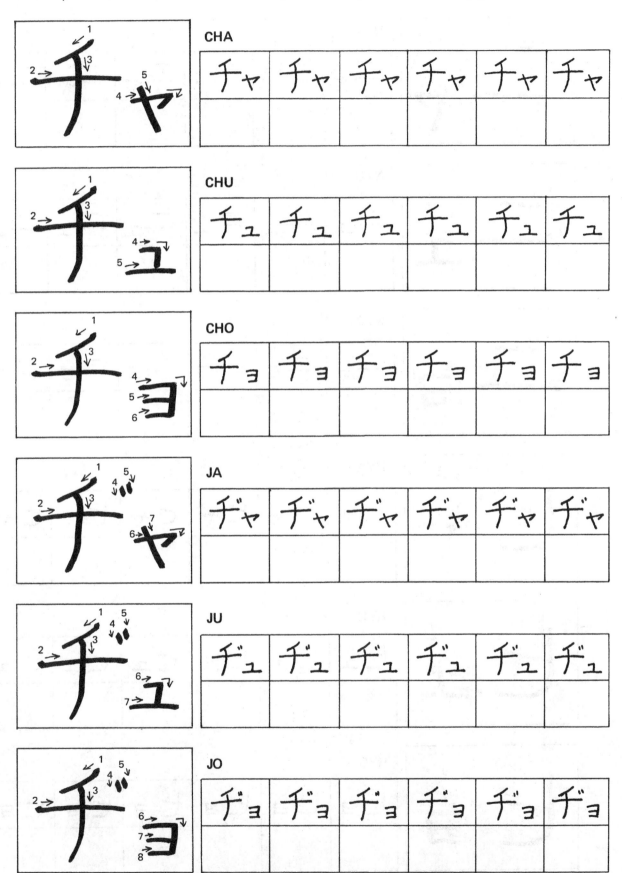

CHA

CHU

CHO

JA

JU

JO

First, **TRACE** each character several times, paying strict attention to stroke order and direction. Then carefully draw the character in the blank squares. Take your time. Develop good habits NOW.

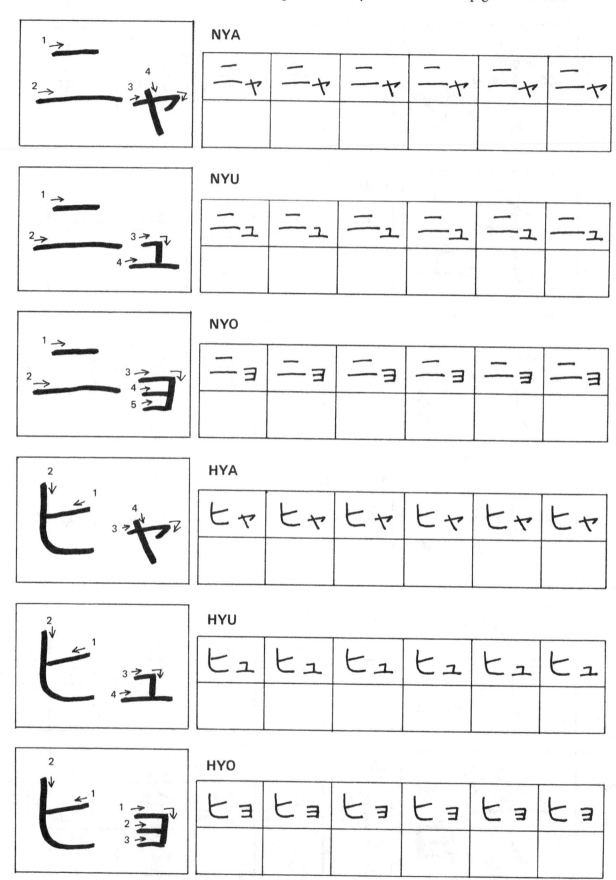

NYA

NYU

NYO

HYA

HYU

HYO

First, **TRACE** each character several times, paying strict attention to stroke order and direction. Then carefully draw the character in the blank squares. Take your time. Develop good habits NOW.

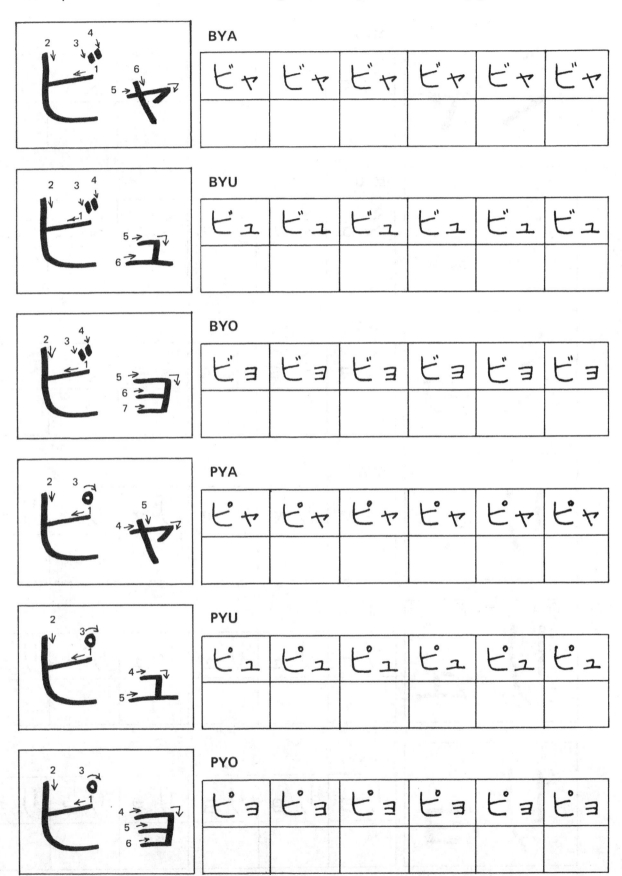

BYA

ビャ	ビャ	ビャ	ビャ	ビャ	ビャ

BYU

ビュ	ビュ	ビュ	ビュ	ビュ	ビュ

BYO

ビョ	ビョ	ビョ	ビョ	ビョ	ビョ

PYA

ピャ	ピャ	ピャ	ピャ	ピャ	ピャ

PYU

ピュ	ピュ	ピュ	ピュ	ピュ	ピュ

PYO

ピョ	ピョ	ピョ	ピョ	ピョ	ピョ

First, **TRACE** each character several times, paying strict attention to stroke order and direction. Then carefully draw the character in the blank squares. Take your time. Develop good habits NOW.

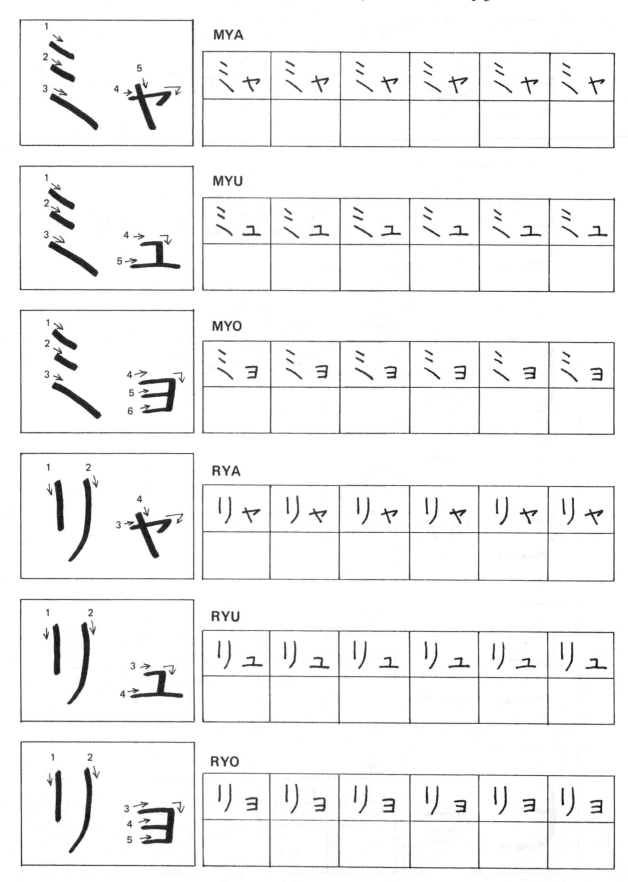

MYA

MYU

MYO

RYA

RYU

RYO

Writing words
in Katakana

Most of the information given in regard to the use of *HIRAGANA* in writing words is true also for *KATAKANA*. This section will teach you the few minor differences, plus some special instructions to help you learn to use *KATAKANA* quickly and correctly.

Before you continue with this section, review pages 29–32 of the section on writing words in *HIRAGANA*. Then come back to this page and proceed with the exercises that follow.

Double consonants

Rules for double consonants are exactly the same in *KATAKANA* as in *HIRAGANA*. Practice writing the examples shown below (first, TRACE, then copy), paying careful attention to the use of the character TSU (ッ).

SUNAKKU
("snack shop")

スナック

ROKETTO
("rocket")

ロケット

HOTTO DOGGU
("hot dog")

ホット　ドッグ

Notice that voiced consonants (as in *HOTTO DOGGU*) may be doubled in *KATAKANA*; whereas, there are no doubled voiced consonants in the Japanese language, and therefore no doubled voiced consonants in *HIRAGANA*.

As with *HIRAGANA*, of course, the double *N* is represented by use of the single-consonant character *N'* (ン).

TONNERU ("tunnel")

トンネル

INNINGU ("inning")

インニング

Long vowels

One major difference between *HIRAGANA* and *KATAKANA* usage is in the representation of long vowels. If you are writing a Japanese word in *KATAKANA*, the exact same rules apply as when writing in *HIRAGANA*; however, if you are writing a non-Japanese word in *KATAKANA*, any vowel may be elongated by writing a dash (—) after it. Note the differences in the Japanese and non-Japanese examples below as you TRACE and then copy each one in the spaces provided.

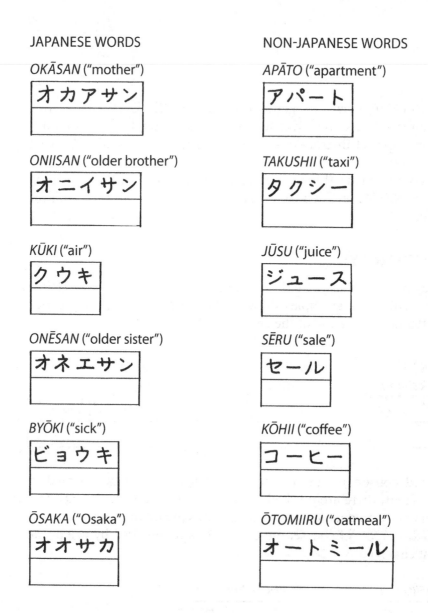

JAPANESE WORDS

OKĀSAN ("mother")
オカアサン

ONIISAN ("older brother")
オニイサン

KŪKI ("air")
クウキ

ONĒSAN ("older sister")
オネエサン

BYŌKI ("sick")
ビョウキ

ŌSAKA ("Osaka")
オオサカ

NON-JAPANESE WORDS

APĀTO ("apartment")
アパート

TAKUSHII ("taxi")
タクシー

JŪSU ("juice")
ジュース

SĒRU ("sale")
セール

KŌHII ("coffee")
コーヒー

ŌTOMIIRU ("oatmeal")
オートミール

When writing vertically in *KATAKANA*, you should write the dash vertically also:

SUKII ("ski")
スキー

SŪPĀ ("super-market")
スーパー

IMĒJI ("image")
イメージ

Mixed languages

When part of a word is from a foreign language and part is Japanese, the foreign portion is written in *KATAKANA*, and the Japanese part in *HIRAGANA* (or *KANJI*). Practice writing the following examples:

AMERIKAJIN ("American")
アメリカじん

DOITSUGO ("German lang.")
ドイツご

RŌMAJI (Roman alphabet)
ローマじ

SOREN (Soviet Union)
ソれん

KASHŪ (California)
カしゅう

KYANPU O SURU ("to camp")
キャンプをする

Abbreviation and creativity

Often a foreign word transliterated into Japanese will become very long and unwieldy, and so it will be abbreviated to make it more comfortable to say. Note the following popular examples:

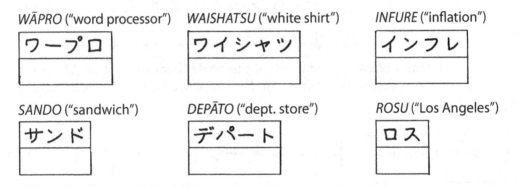

WĀPRO ("word processor")
ワープロ

WAISHATSU ("white shirt")
ワイシャツ

INFURE ("inflation")
インフレ

SANDO ("sandwich")
サンド

DEPĀTO ("dept. store")
デパート

ROSU ("Los Angeles")
ロス

Also, because there are many foreign language sounds and sound combinations that do not exist in Japanese, *KATAKANA* must sometimes be used very creatively to approximate the foreign sound most accurately. Practice writing the words below, paying special attention to how the foreign sound combinations are represented.

ŪRU ("wool")
ウール

UŌTĀ ("water")
ウォーター

DIZUNIIRANDO ("Disneyland")
ディズニーランド

FuASSHON ("fashion")
ファッション

FuŌKU ("fork")
フォーク

FuIRUMU ("film")
フィルム

(NOTE: Words such as these are usually either written in *KATAKANA* or spelled the usual English way, rather than romanized character for character as above.)

Of course, when there are two or more foreign words together, especially in a person's full name or the name of a company, it may be difficult to tell where one word ends and the next begins. The Japanese will often use a solid dot (•), centered in the space between the words or names, to indicate the break. Practice the following names in the spaces provided.

HOTTO DOGGU ("hot dog")   MIKKII MAUSU ("M. Mouse")   JON SUMISU ("John Smith")

ホット・ドッグ | ミッキー・マウス | ジョン・スミス

FORŌ ZA RĪDĀ ("Follow the Leader")   NASHONAL SĀBISU ("National Service [Co.]")

フォロー・ザ・リーダー | ナショナル・サービス

Note that when a foreign name is written with the person's middle initial, the initial is written in *RŌMAJI* and usually separated from the other two names by a solid dot, as in:

JON G. SUMISU ("John G. Smith")

ジョン・G・スミス

Foreign names often require creativity to write them in *KATAKANA*. Try to guess what common Western names are written in *KATAKANA* below. (Correct answers are given in Appendix C.)

1. デービッド	2. レイモンド	3. キャロリン
4. シャーリー	5. スミス	6. ジョンソン
7. アンダーソン	8. トンプソン	9. ロバーツ
10. ホワイト	11. カーター	12. ランプキン

Keep in mind that relatively few foreign words used by the Japanese have been standardized as to how they may be written in *KATAKANA*, and you may find some of the examples presented here written slightly differently. Names, in particular, may be represented in various ways.

Writing sentences
in Katakana

Although *KATAKANA* is used primarily for words of foreign origin, it is possible to use it for anything Japanese as well. The rules for writing sentences are exactly the same for *KATAKANA* as for *HIRAGANA*, including the particles, spaces, punctuation, underlining, etc., with one exception; that is, the repetition symbols taught on page 37 are not used for words of foreign origin.

Review the information given on pages 33–37, then proceed with the exercises that follow in the practice and self-test section.

Katakana practice and self-test

On the following pages are exercises to help you practice reading and writing in *KATAKANA*.

Follow the instructions carefully. Some of the exercises require that you TRACE, COPY, and then ROMANIZE sentences given for you in *KATAKANA*. Other exercises require that you write in *KATAKANA* sentences that are presented in *RŌMAJI*.

In some exercises, the *KATAKANA* is presented in machine-made characters; in others it is handwritten. Some exercises are written horizontally; some are written vertically. Every effort has been made to give you experience in a variety of writing situations, as well as to expose you to some slightly different handwriting styles.

After you have finished each exercise, check your work carefully against the correct responses given in Appendix C in the back of this book. Translations of the sentences used in this section are given in Appendix D.

First, TRACE the following sentences, then COPY them, character for character, in the first blank space for each line. In the second blank space, ROMANIZE what you have written.

trace	リ タ ナ カ サ ン　　ハ　　ド ノ　　ヨ ウ　　ナ
copy	
rōmaji	

trace	ヒ ト　　デ ス　　カ。²⟩ ワ タ ク シ　　ハ
copy	
rōmaji	

trace	チ イ サ イ　　ア パ ー ト　　ニ　　ス ン デ
copy	
rōmaji	

trace	イ マ ス。³⟩ シ ャ チ ョ ウ サ ン　　ハ　　ス テ キ
copy	
rōmaji	

trace	ナ　　ヒ ト　　デ ス　　ネ。⁴⟩ サ ク バ ン
copy	
rōmaji	

trace	ノ　　カ イ　　ハ　　オ ソ カ ッ タ　　デ ス
copy	
rōmaji	

trace	カ。⁵⟩ コ ノ　　ダ イ ガ ク　　ニ　　ハ　　ド ノ
copy	
rōmaji	

trace	ヨ ウ　　ナ　　ヒ ト　　ガ　　イ マ ス　　カ。
copy	
rōmaji	

Check your work against correct responses given in Appendix C.

First, TRACE the following sentences, then COPY them, character for character, in the first blank space for each line. In the second blank space, ROMANIZE what you have written.

リ¹⁾タナカサン　ハ　ケサ　ナンジニ

キマシタ　カ。²⁾ワタクシ　ハ　シャ

チョウサン　ガ　ハワイ　ニ　イク

ト　オモイマス。³⁾カレ　ガ　ハチ

ジ　マデ　マット　オモイマセン。

⁴⁾モウ　デンワ　ヲ　シタ　ト　オ

モイマス。⁵⁾オカアサン　ハ　マダ

カイモノ　ヲ　シマセン　デシタ。

Check your work against correct responses given in Appendix C.

First, TRACE the following sentences, then COPY them, character for character, in the first blank space for each line. In the second blank space, ROMANIZE what you have written.

1) リ ワタクシ ハ ハンカガイ ニ イ

ッテ カイモノ ヲ シマシタ。 2) ハ

ワイ ニ イク トキ トモダチ ノ

ウチ ニ トマリマス。 3) エイガ ヲ

ミル コト ガ スキ デス。 4) オ

カアサン ハ ソコ ニ イッテ カ

エリマシタ。 5) キャンプ ヲ スル コ

ト ハ タノシイ ト オモイマス。

Check your work against correct responses given in Appendix C.

First, TRACE the following sentences, then COPY them, character for character, in the first blank space for each line. In the second blank space, ROMANIZE what you have written.

trace	ソ ム コ ウ ニ ス ワ ッ テ イ ル ヒ ト
copy	
rōmaji	

trace	ハ ダ レ デ ス カ。 ²⁾コ ン バ ン
copy	
rōmaji	

trace	エ イ ガ ニ イ キ タ イ ト オ モ イ
copy	
rōmaji	

trace	マ ス。 ³⁾ワ タ ク シ ハ ト モ ダ チ
copy	
rōmaji	

trace	ト ベ ン キョ ウ シ タ イ ト オ モ イ
copy	
rōmaji	

trace	マ ス。 ⁴⁾キョ ウ シ ツ デ ハ ナ シ タ
copy	
rōmaji	

trace	ヒ ト ハ ダ レ デ シ タ カ。 ⁵⁾キ
copy	
rōmaji	

trace	ノ ウ ナ ニ モ シ タ ク ナ カ ッ タ デ ス。
copy	
rōmaji	

Check your work against correct responses given in Appendix C.

First, TRACE the following sentences, then COPY them, character for character, in the first blank space for each line. In the second blank space, ROMANIZE what you have written.

trace / copy / rōmaji	リ チョット ハナシテ モ イイ デス

trace / copy / rōmaji	カ。 ²⁾ アシタ マデ デンワ シ

trace / copy / rōmaji	ナクテ モ イイ デス カ。 ³⁾ 木

trace / copy / rōmaji	ンヤ デ タベテ ハ イケマセン。

trace / copy / rōmaji	⁴⁾ シャチョウサン ト ハナサナクテ

trace / copy / rōmaji	ハ イケマセン。 ⁵⁾ マイニチ クス

trace / copy / rōmaji	リ ヲ ノマナクテ ハ ダメ デ

trace / copy / rōmaji	ス。 ⁶⁾ モウ カエッテ モ イイ デス。

Check your work against correct responses given in Appendix C.

First, TRACE the following sentences, then COPY them, character for character, in the blank space to the right of each line. Then ROMANIZE them on the blank horizontal lines at the bottom.

trace	copy	trace	copy	trace	copy	trace	copy	trace	copy	trace	copy	trace	copy	trace	copy
コドモ ハ ヒジョウ ニ カシコイ デス。		10. シゴト ハ タクサン アリマシタ カラ、オソクナリマシタ。 11. アノ		9. オトウサン ハ カレ ガ スキ デス ノデ、カネモチ ニ シマシタ。		リ ヤスクナイ デス。 8. カノジョ ハ ケサ ビョウキ ニ ナリマシタ。		ウイ アパート ニ スンデ イマス カ。 7. ベンリ デス ガ アマ		クナイ デス、ネ。 5. タナカサン ハ ゲンキ ナ ヒト デス。 6. ド		ジョ ノ オネエサン ハ ウツクシイ デス ケレドモ、アマリ ヤサシ		ムズカシカッタ デス。 3. キョウ ハ スゴク サムイ デス。 4. カノ		アナタ ノ クルマ ハ オオキイ デス カ。 2. キノウ ノ テスト ハ	

1. ↙

Romanize:

_____

_____

_____

_____

_____

_____

_____

Check your work against the correct responses in Appendix C.

First, TRACE the following sentences, then COPY them, character for character, in the blank space to the right of each line. Then ROMANIZE them on the blank horizontal lines at the bottom.

trace	copy	trace	copy	trace	copy	trace	copy	trace	copy	trace	copy	trace	copy	trace	copy
シマシタ カ。11. ケサ ゴハン ヲ タベテ、ガッコウ ヘ イキマシタ。		ジョウズ デハナイ ト オモイマス。10. キョウ アナタ ハ ナニ ヲ		ベテ イナカッタ ト イイマシタ。9. カレ ノ ニホンゴ ハ アマリ		タ ガ、ナニモ カイマセン デシタ。8. カレラ ガ トモダチ ト タ		ニ イッタ ト イイマシタ。7. トウキョウ ノ デパート ヘ イキマシ		ハ トショカン デハナイ ト オモイマス。6. カノジョ ハ ニホン		シタ。4. オカネ ガ ナイ カラ、カイモノ ガ デキマセン。5. コレ		ヨリ、ナレ ヨ。3. カノジョ ハ リンゴ ガ スキ ダ ト イイマ		オレンジイロ ノ ハナ モ キイロ ノ ハナ モ アリマス。2. ナラウ	

1.

Romanize:

_____

_____

_____

_____

_____

_____

_____

Check your work against the correct responses in Appendix C.

First, TRACE the following sentences, then COPY them, character for character, in the blank space to the right of each line. Then ROMANIZE them on the blank horizontal lines at the bottom.

1.

| trace | copy | trace | copy | trace | copy | trace | copy | trace | copy | trace | copy | trace | copy | trace | copy | trace | copy |

ニホンショク ヲ タベタクナカッタ カラ、 トモダチ ト ショクドウ ヘ イキマセン デシタ。

2. アナタ ハ ナンジ ニ タベタイ ト オモイマス カ。

3. ヨジ マデ ニ デンワ ヲ シナクテ ハ イケナイ ト オモイマス。

4. モウ デンワ ヲ シテ モ イイ デス カ。

5. ヨク ガンバラナクテ ハ ダメ デス ヨ。

6. ココ デ タバコ ヲ ノンデ モ イイ ト オモイマス カ。

7. ナニモ シナクテ モ イイ デス カ。

8. オトモダチ ガ ウンテン シテ ハ ダメ デス。

9. オトウサン ガ コナクテ ハ イケマセン。

10. キョウ モ アシタ モ ベンキョウ シナクテ ハ イケマセン。

Romanize: _____

_____

_____

_____

_____

_____

_____

Check your work against the correct responses in Appendix C.

First, TRACE the following sentences, then COPY them, character for character, in the blank space to the right of each line. Then ROMANIZE them on the blank horizontal lines at the bottom.

1.

trace	copy	trace	copy	trace	copy	trace	copy	trace	copy	trace	copy	trace	copy	trace	copy

1. フユ ニ ナッテ、スキー ヲ シマシタ。
2. アノ ヒト ハ ニホンジン デ エイゴ ガ デキマセン。
3. カレラ ハ イッショウケンメイ ニ ハタライテ イマス。
4. シャチョウサン ハ ヒジョウ ニ タイセツナ ヨウジ ガ アル ト イイマシタ。
5. カノジョ ハ ホントウ ニ キレイ デス。
6. コンバン ワタクシ ハ エイガ ニ イキタイ ト オモイマス ガ イッショ ニ イッテ クダサイマセン カ。
7. タノシミ ニ シテ イマス。
8. ユウビンキョク デ ハタライテ イル キレイナ オンナ ノ ヒト ハ ダレ デス カ。
9. ワタクシ ハ キョウナニモ シタクナイト オモイマス。

Romanize:

_____

_____

_____

_____

_____

_____

_____

_____

Check your work against the correct responses in Appendix C.

First, COPY each line below onto the first blank space beneath it. In the second blank space write the line in *RŌMAJI*. Check your work carefully against Appendix C.

1. アイス・クリーム を たべましょう か。　2. きのう の

copy _____

rōmaji _____

テスト は むずかしかった です、ネ!　3. この アパー

copy _____

rōmaji _____

ト は あまり べんり では ありません。　4. アパート

copy _____

rōmaji _____

を きれい に して ください。　5. オレンジいろ の く

copy _____

rōmaji _____

るま は わたくし の です。　6. アメリカじん は いつ

copy _____

rōmaji _____

も サンドイッチ を たべる と いいました。　7. かれ

copy _____

rōmaji _____

は サン・フランシスコ へ いきました けれども、ロス

copy _____

rōmaji _____

へ いきません でした。　8. テレビ を みて いた とき、

copy _____

rōmaji _____

ポップコーン を たべました。

copy _____

rōmaji _____

First, COPY each line below onto the first blank space beneath it. In the second blank space write the line in *RŌMAJI*. Check your work carefully against Appendix C.

1. おにいさん は ニュー・ヨーク に すんで います が、

copy _____

rōmaji _____

フランス で べんきょう しました。 2. やま まで ヒッ

copy _____

rōmaji _____

チハイク を して、 キャンプ を しました。 3. ハワイ

copy _____

rōmaji _____

へ いく とき、 ホノルル の ホテル に とまります。

copy _____

rōmaji _____

4. ホワイトさん は スペインじん の おともだち が ら

copy _____

rōmaji _____

いしゅう くる と いいました。 5. いま L・A・タイム

copy _____

rōmaji _____

ズ を よんで いる ひと は スミスさん です。 6. しろ

copy _____

rōmaji _____

い セーター を きて いる ハワイじん は 「スター・ウ

copy _____

rōmaji _____

ォーズ」 と いう えいが を みて きました。

copy _____

rōmaji _____

Write the following sentences completely in *KATAKANA*. Check your work carefully against the correct responses given in Appendix C.

1. TANAKA-SAN WA GENKI NA HITO DESU, NE.

2. DŌ IU APĀTO NI SUNDE IMASU KA.

3. BENRI DESU GA, AMARI ŌKIKUNAI DESU.

4. KYŌ WA HAYAKU ATSUKUNARIMASHITA.

5. MUKŌ NO OTOKO NO HITO WA ISSHŌKENMEI NI HATARAITE IMASU.

6. KAI WA ZENZEN OMOSHIROKUNAKATTA DESU YO.

7. ANATA WA NIHONSHOKU GA SUKI DESU KA?

8. ICHIBAN SUKI NA IRO WA NANIIRO DESU KA?

9. ONIISAN WA KINŌ UCHI NI KAETTA TOKI, NANI O SHIMASHITA KA?

10. BUCHŌ-SAN GA ATARASHII KURUMA O KATTA TO IIMASHITA.

11. KANOJO WA UTAU KOTO GA DEKIRU TO OMOIMASEN.

12. KARE NO KURUMA GA AKAI TO ITTA TO OMOIMASU.

Write the following sentences completely in *KATAKANA*. Check your work carefully against the correct responses given in Appendix C.

1. KARE WA KYŌ SHIGOTO NI IKANAKATTA DESU.

2. ANO HITO WA JIMUSHO NI KONAKATTA TO OMOIMASU.

3. SAKUBAN NO KAI WA NAGAKUNAKUTE YOKATTA DESU.

4. ANO HON WA BETSU NI OMOSHIROKUNAI DESU.

5. DOYŌBI WATAKUSHI WA OJIISAN NO TOKORO E IKIMASHITA.

6. KANOJO WA MAINICHI DAIGAKU DE HATARAKIMASU.

7. ANATA WA NANI GA HOSHII TO OMOIMASU KA?

8. ENPITSU GA HITSUYŌ DA TO IIMASHITA.

9. ANO HITO WA EKI O SAGASHITE IRU TO IIMASHITA.

10. HON'YA E ITTE, OKĀSAN NO TANONDA HON O KAIMASHITA.

11. MŌ KAETTE MO II DESU KA?

12. GETSUYŌBI NI MATA GAKKŌ E IKANAKEREBA NARIMASEN.

Write the following sentences completely in *KANA*, using *KATAKANA* for words of foreign origin and *HIRAGANA* for everything else. Check your work carefully against the correct responses given in Appendix C.

1. *SUMISU SENSEI NO ONĒSAN WA HAWAI NI SUNDE IMASU.*

2. *WATAKUSHI NO KAMERA WA DAME NI NARIMASHITA.*

3. *MAZUI HANBĀGĀ O TABEMASHITA NODE, BYŌKI NI NARIMASHITA.*

4. *ORENJIIRO NO SĒTĀ O KITE IRU HITO WA O-TOMODACHI DESU KA?*

5. *KARE WA AMERIKA NO GINKŌ DE HATARAITE IMASU.*

6. *ASHITA DEPĀTO E ITTE, MIKKII MAUSU NO TOKEI O KAIMASU.*

7. *TOMODACHI WA FURANSU NO DAIGAKU DE BENKYŌ SHITE IMASU.*

8. *RANCHI GA OWATTE, SŪPĀ NI IKITAI TO OMOIMASU.*

9. *OKĀSAN WA BASU DE HANKAGAI E IKIMASHITA.*

10. *SUTĒKI TO SARADA O CHŪMON SHIMASHITA KA?*

11. *KOKO DE TABAKO O NONDE MO II DESU KA?*

12. *EIGAKAN NI ITTE, "SHINDERERA" TO IU EIGA O MIMASHITA.*

Write the following sentences completely in *KANA*, using *KATAKANA* for words of foreign origin and *HIRAGANA* for everything else. Check your work carefully against the correct responses given in Appendix C.

1. ANO PEN WA JŪ-DORU YONJŪGO-SENTO DE TAKAI DESU.

2. KARE WA SUĒDENJIN DE, FURANSUGO TO DOITSUGO O HANASHIMASU.

3. IMA SUKII O SHITE INAI HITO WA BYŌKI DESU KA?

4. AISU KURIIMU GA DAISUKI DE, MAINICHI TABEMASU.

5. SUNAKKU E ITTE, SANDOITCHI O TABEMASHŌ KA?

6. TAKUSHII DE ITTE KIMASHITA KA?

7. SĒRU GA ATTA KARA, OKĀSAN WA SŪPĀ NI IKIMASHITA.

8. GASORIN GA NAI KARA, KURUMA O UNTEN DEKIMASEN.

9. NANPĒJI MADE YOMIMASHITA KA?

10. RAJIO O KIITE IRU HITO WA MEKISHIKOJIN DA TO OMOIMASU.

11. SUMISU-SAN TO BURAUN-SAN WA YŌROPPA DE RYOKŌ O SHITE IMASU.

12. HOTERU NO RESUTORAN DE SHOKUJI O SHIMASHITA.

PART THREE

Practice exercises
and self-tests

Before beginning these exercises, reread the overview on pages vii–viii, as well as specific instructions on pages 15–16 (voiced vs. voiceless consonants), 21–22 (combination characters), 29–31 (double consonants), 31–32 (long vowels), 33–37 (particles and punctuation), 81–84 (*KATAKANA*), plus *KANA* exceptions in Appendix B.

Always check your work against the correct responses in Appendix C. For translations of individual sentences and paragraphs, see Appendix D.

On pages 129–130 is a writing grid that you should find helpful in improving your handwriting as you practice. The grid can be used for both horizontal and vertical writing practice.

Tips for making the best use of these exercises

- **Using the writing grid** (pp. 129–130). Because of the overall complex nature of Japanese writing, particularly *KANJI*, the "white space" around each character helps keep your writing legible. Many students of Japanese tend to write the characters much closer together than native Japanese are taught to do. Practicing writing *KANA* on a copy of the grid will help you develop good writing/spacing habits. It is a good idea to practice an exercise on regular lined paper, as well, then compare your writing with what you wrote in the grid.
- **Horizontal vs. vertical.** Although the exercises in this section are presented in a horizontal format, you should also practice writing each exercise vertically. Both formats are used extensively in Japanese written works.
- **Spaces.** Remember that, although spaces are not normally used between words when writing with *KANJI*, when writing in *KANA* the spaces are helpful to clarify where words begin and end. In this book we also use spaces to make it easier for students to look up words they don't know. Ordinarily a particle after a word might not be offset with a space, and two-part verbs like *KAITE IMASU* might be written as one word, even when no *KANJI* is included.
- **Writing implement.** Try your handwriting with a variety of writing implements. You may find it easier to make your characters more "native-looking" if you use a sharp pencil, a fountain pen, or a gel-type pen, rather than a ball-point pen or a marker. And don't forget to hold your pen or pencil upright, as if writing with a brush.

- **Tracing.** Although tracing exercises are not included in this practice exercise section, it is a good idea to do some tracing from time to time. Just as in artwork, tracing the characters will improve your skills much more quickly, training your hand to make each stroke look as it should for both legibility and correctness, as well as proportion and spacing.
- **Review stroke order.** It is also a good idea to review stroke order of individual characters before beginning this section of exercises to make sure you are developing correct habits. Developing good habits with *KANA* will be a great help when you advance to writing *KANJI*.

Hiragana-only exercises

Writing words

READ each of the following words and ROMANIZE it on the first line below it. CHECK your work against Appendix C; then cover the original words and REWRITE them in *HIRAGANA* on the second line beneath each. CHECK your *KANA* against the originals.

あえる (can meet)
_____
_____

あおぞら (blue sky)
_____
_____

あいさつ (greeting)
_____
_____

えんぴつ (pencil)
_____
_____

えいえん (eternal)
_____
_____

えほん (picture book)
_____
_____

いだい (great)
_____
_____

のべる (to speak out)
_____
_____

うすい (thin)
_____
_____

おりる (to descend)
_____
_____

うえる (to plant)
_____
_____

けいけん (experience)
_____
_____

おいしい (delicious)
_____
_____

さがす (to look for)
_____
_____

せんせい (teacher)
_____
_____

こくせき (nationality)
_____
_____

ごみ (trash)
_____
_____

こころ (heart/mind)
_____
_____

ぎんこう (bank)
_____
_____

きかい (opportunity)
_____
_____

ぐんじん (soldier)
_____
_____

げんき (healthy)
_____
_____

しつれい (rude)
_____
_____

がいこく (foreign country)
_____
_____

ぎもん (question)
_____
_____

つなみ (tsunami)
_____
_____

なまえ (name)
_____
_____

ざっし (magazine)
_____
_____

とうちゃく (arrival)
_____
_____

でかける (to go out)
_____
_____

はいる (to enter)
_____
_____

おばけ (ghost)
_____
_____

びんぼう (poverty)
_____
_____

べんり (convenient)
_____
_____

きっぷ (ticket)
_____
_____

ぼく (I, me [casual])
_____
_____

ぽっくり (suddenly)
_____
_____

いそぐ (to hurry)
_____
_____

ずつう (headache)
_____
_____

どく (poison)
_____
_____

おくりもの (gift)
_____
_____

かなづち (hammer)
_____
_____

ぬすむ (to steal)
_____
_____

ひみつ (secret)
_____
_____

ばつ (punishment)
_____
_____

ぜんぶ (all)
_____
_____

かっぱつ (lively)
_____
_____

てっぺん (summit)
_____
_____

まるい (round)
_____
_____

むすぶ (to tie up)
_____
_____

じしょ (dictionary)
_____
_____

ちかてつ (subway)
_____
_____

ねつ (fever)
_____
_____

だめ (bad, useless)
_____
_____

てつだい (help)
_____
_____

のみもの (drink)
_____
_____

へび (snake)
_____
_____

おおい (plentiful)
_____
_____

わんぱく (naughty)
_____
_____

ぴったり (exactly)
_____
_____

べんとう (box lunch)
_____
_____

みち (path)
_____
_____

めぐみ (blessing)
_____
_____

こんげつ (this month)
_____
_____

せんしゅう (last week)
_____
_____

そくたつ (special delivery)
_____
_____

ぜんぜん (not at all)
_____
_____

ちぢめる (to shorten)
_____
_____

ときどき (sometimes)
_____
_____

にちようび (Sunday)
_____
_____

ふつう (usual/normal)
_____
_____

ほんぶ (head office)
_____
_____

じゅんび (preparation)
_____
_____

ぶんぽう (grammar)
_____
_____

げっぷ (monthly payment)
_____
_____

こんぽん (basic)
_____
_____

めんどう (nuisance)
_____
_____

むら (village)
_____
_____

おもさ (weight)
_____
_____

やきめし (fried rice)
_____
_____

もはん (example)
_____
_____

かんむり (crown)
_____
_____

やちん (house rent)
_____
_____

やくだつ (to be helpful)
_____
_____

やすい (cheap)
_____
_____

おおや (landlord)
_____
_____

ゆき (snow)
_____
_____

ゆれる (to tremble)
_____
_____

さゆう (right & left)
_____
_____

よあけ (dawn)
_____
_____

かり (hunting)
_____
_____

ようしょく (Western food)
_____
_____

からだ (body)
_____
_____

へいわ (peace)
_____
_____

あかるい (bright)
_____
_____

らいねん (next year)
_____
_____

りっぱ (splendid)
_____
_____

れきし (history)
_____
_____

はれる (to clear up)
_____
_____

るす (away from home)
_____
_____

だんろ (fireplace)
_____
_____

わかい (young)
_____
_____

ぎゃく (reverse)
_____
_____

ろうじん (old person)
_____
_____

りょこう (travel)
_____
_____

きょうみ (interest)
_____
_____

ぎゅうにく (beef)
_____
_____

ざんねん (regrettable)
_____
_____

みょうじ (surname)
_____
_____

びょうき (sick)
_____
_____

ちょうど (exactly)
_____
_____

きゅうじつ (holiday)
_____
_____

ちゃいろ (brown)
_____
_____

しゃしん (photograph)
_____
_____

きゃく (guest)
_____
_____

ぎゅうにゅう (milk)
_____
_____

りょうしん (parents)
_____
_____

にゅうがく (to enter school)
_____
_____

ちゅうしょく (lunch)
_____
_____

ぎょせん (fishing boat)
_____
_____

りゃく (abbreviation)
_____
_____

にゅうじょう (admission)
_____
_____

りょうり (cooking)
_____
_____

りゅうがく (study abroad)
_____
_____

Writing sentences

READ each sentence several times, then ROMANIZE them on the lines below each. CHECK your romanization against the correct responses in Appendix C. Then cover the original sentence and REWRITE it in *HIRAGANA* on a copy of the writing grid (pp. 129–130). CHECK your *KANA* sentence against the original. (Translations of all sentences are in Appendix D.)

け	さ		あ	め		が		よ	く		ふ	っ	て		い	ま	し	た	
が	、	じ	ゅ	う	に	じ		ご	ろ		に		は	れ	て	、	い	ま	
は		ど	こ	も		あ	お	ぞ	ら		で	す	。						

Rōmaji: _____

_____

_____

き	の	う		が	っ	こ	う		が		お	わ	っ	て		か	ら		と
も	だ	ち		の		う	ち		へ		い	っ	て	、		ゆ	う	し	ょ	く
を		ご	ち	そ	う		に		な	り	ま	し	た	。					

Rōmaji: _____

_____

_____

| あ | し | た | | は | | き | ゅ | う | じ | つ | | で | す | | か | ら | 、 | ど | こ |
| か | | へ | | い | き | ま | し | ょ | う | | か | 。 | | | | | | | |

Rōmaji: _____

_____

| ざ | っ | し | | も | | し | ん | ぶ | ん | | も | | あ | り | ま | す | | が | 、 |
| ど | ち | ら | | を | | よ | み | た | い | | で | す | | か | 。 | | | | |

Rōmaji: _____

_____

| し | ん | じ | ゅ | く | | え | き | | は | | ひ | と | | が | | い | っ | ぱ | い |
| で | す | | か | ら | 、 | と | て | も | | に | ぎ | や | か | | で | す | 。 | | |

Rōmaji: _____

_____

は	る	や	す	み		に		で	ん	し	ゃ		で		り	ょ	こ	う	
し	た		こ	と		を		に	っ	き		に		か	き	ま	し	た	。

Rōmaji: _____

は	ち	が	つ		の		じ	ゅ	う	い	ち	に	ち		か	ら		か	い
し	ゃ		が		よ	っ	か	か	ん		や	す	み		に		な	り	ま
す		の	で	、	お	き	な	わ		へ		い	き	た	い		で	す	。

Rōmaji: _____

ら	い	げ	つ		が	っ	こ	う		の		し	け	ん		が		は	じ
ま	り	ま	す		の	で	、	こ	れ	か	ら		ず	っ	と		べ	ん	き
ょ	う		し	な	け	れ	ば		な	り	ま	せ	ん	。					

Rōmaji: _____

し	ょ	う	が	っ	こ	う		の		ま	え		で		あ	か	い		ぼ
う	し		を		か	ぶ	っ	た		お	ん	な		の		ひ	と		は
こ	ど	も		を		ま	っ	て		い	ま	し	た	。					

Rōmaji: _____

お	か	あ	さ	ん		に		て	が	み		を		か	き	た	い		け
れ	ど	も	、	え	ん	ぴ	つ		が		あ	り	ま	せ	ん		の	で	、
か	し	て		く	だ	さ	い	ま	す		か	。							

Rōmaji: _____

け	ん	さ	ん		は		は	こ		の		な	か		を		さ	が	す
と	、	ふ	た	つ		の		お	お	き	い		じ	ゃ	が	い	も		と
に	ん	じ	ん		を		い	っ	ぽ	ん		み	つ	け	ま	し	た	。	

Rōmaji: _____

Writing paragraphs

READ each paragraph several times, then ROMANIZE them on the lines below each. CHECK your romanization against the correct responses in Appendix C. Then cover the original paragraph and REWRITE it in *HIRAGANA* on a copy of the writing grid (pp. 129–130). CHECK your *HIRAGANA* paragraph against the original. (Translations of all paragraphs are in Appendix D.)

に	ほ	ん		の		し	き		は		は	る		と		な	つ		と	
あ	き		と		ふ	ゆ		で	す	。	は	る		は		あ	め		が	
よ	く		ふ	っ	て	、	は	な		が		さ	き	ま	す	。	な	つ		は
あ	つ	い		で	す		か	ら	、	ひ	と		は		う	み		へ		よ
く		で	か	け	ま	す	。	あ	き		が		く	る		と	、	き		の
は	は		こ	う	よ	う		し	ま	す	。	そ	れ	か	ら		さ	む	く	
な	り	、	ゆ	き		が		ふ	り	ま	す	。	い	ち	ば	ん		す	き	
な		き	せ	つ		は		ど	れ		で	す		か	。					

Rōmaji: _____

_____

_____

_____

_____

_____

わ	た	し	た	ち		の		に	わ		の		ま	ん	な	か		に	、	お
お	き	い		ゆ	き	だ	る	ま		が		あ	り	ま	す	。	お	に	い	さ
ん		と		わ	た	し		が		つ	く	っ	た		も	の		で	す	。	
わ	た	し		は		ふ	る	い		ぼ	う	し		を		ゆ	き	だ	る	ま
の		あ	た	ま		に		お	き	ま	し	た	。	お	に	い	さ	ん		が
き	っ	た		き		の		え	だ		は		ゆ	き	だ	る	ま		の	
う	で		に		な	り	ま	し	た	。	お	か	あ	さ	ん		は		し	ゃ
し	ん		を		と	っ	て		く	れ	ま	し	た	。						

Rōmaji: _____

_____

_____

_____

_____

_____

_____

ちちは だいくで、かなづちや のこぎりを よく つかいます。ははは こうとうがっこうで すうがくを おしえて います。あねは かんごふで、びょういんで はたらいて います。あには だいがくせいで、しょうらい ぎんこうの じゅうやくに なりたい です。ぼくは きゅうきゅうしゃの うんてんしゅに なりたいと おもいます。

Rōmaji: _____

_____

_____

_____

_____

_____

_____

_____

どうぶつえんに いった こと が ありますか。いろいろ な どうぶつ が いて、おもしろい ところ です。とら も くま も いて、ぞう や きりん も、ちいさい とり も、へび も います。わたし の いちばん すき な どうぶつ は しまうま です。らいしゅう かぞく と いっしょ に ひがしやま どうぶつえん に いきます。

Rōmaji: _____

_____

_____

_____

_____

_____

_____

きんようびに おとうさんは、「あした こうえんに いこうか」と いいました。みんな「はい、いこうよ」と さけびました。つぎの あさ、みんなで でんしゃに のって やまの こうえんへ でかけました。やまの したから ながい かいだんが うえまで つづきます。いちじかん のぼって、やっと ちょうじょうに とうちゃく しました。

Rōmaji: _____

_____

_____

_____

_____

_____

_____

_____

うちの ちかくに ひろい かわが あります。かわの そばには あひるが います。おやは にわで、こどもは ごわ います。まいしゅう にちようびに うちの おねえさんと あひるの かぞくを みに いきます。いじめませんから、あひるは こわがりません。こんどの にちようび、たべものを もって いきます。

Rōmaji: _____

_____

_____

_____

_____

_____

_____

<table>
<tr><td>き</td><td>の</td><td>う</td><td></td><td>お</td><td>じ</td><td>い</td><td>さ</td><td>ん</td><td></td><td>の</td><td></td><td>う</td><td>ち</td><td></td><td>へ</td><td></td><td>い</td><td>き</td><td>ま</td><td>し</td></tr>
<tr><td>た</td><td>。</td><td>お</td><td>じ</td><td>い</td><td>さ</td><td>ん</td><td></td><td>は</td><td></td><td>ち</td><td>ょ</td><td>っ</td><td>と</td><td></td><td>と</td><td>し</td><td></td><td>を</td><td></td><td>と</td></tr>
<tr><td>っ</td><td>て</td><td></td><td>い</td><td>ま</td><td>す</td><td></td><td>が</td><td>、</td><td>と</td><td>て</td><td>も</td><td></td><td>た</td><td>の</td><td>し</td><td>い</td><td></td><td>ひ</td><td>と</td><td></td></tr>
<tr><td>だ</td><td></td><td>と</td><td></td><td>お</td><td>も</td><td>い</td><td>ま</td><td>す</td><td>。</td><td>す</td><td>ご</td><td>く</td><td></td><td>ふ</td><td>る</td><td>い</td><td></td><td>く</td><td>る</td><td>ま</td></tr>
<tr><td>を</td><td></td><td>も</td><td>っ</td><td>て</td><td></td><td>い</td><td>ま</td><td>す</td><td>。</td><td>お</td><td>じ</td><td>い</td><td>さ</td><td>ん</td><td></td><td>と</td><td></td><td>お</td><td>ば</td><td>あ</td></tr>
<tr><td>さ</td><td>ん</td><td></td><td>は</td><td></td><td>た</td><td>び</td><td>た</td><td>び</td><td></td><td>く</td><td>る</td><td>ま</td><td></td><td>で</td><td></td><td>ど</td><td>こ</td><td>か</td><td></td><td>へ</td></tr>
<tr><td>あ</td><td>そ</td><td>び</td><td></td><td>に</td><td></td><td>い</td><td>き</td><td>ま</td><td>す</td><td>。</td><td>き</td><td>の</td><td>う</td><td></td><td>さ</td><td>ん</td><td>に</td><td>ん</td><td></td><td>で</td></tr>
<tr><td>と</td><td>な</td><td>り</td><td></td><td>の</td><td></td><td>ま</td><td>ち</td><td></td><td>に</td><td></td><td>く</td><td>る</td><td>ま</td><td></td><td>で</td><td></td><td>い</td><td>っ</td><td>て</td><td></td></tr>
<tr><td>き</td><td>ま</td><td>し</td><td>た</td><td>。</td><td></td><td></td><td></td><td></td><td></td><td></td><td></td><td></td><td></td><td></td><td></td><td></td><td></td><td></td><td></td><td></td></tr>
</table>

Rōmaji: _____

_____

_____

_____

_____

_____

_____

<table>
<tr><td>せ</td><td>ん</td><td>し</td><td>ゅ</td><td>う</td><td></td><td>お</td><td>お</td><td>さ</td><td>か</td><td></td><td>へ</td><td></td><td>ひ</td><td>こ</td><td>う</td><td>き</td><td></td><td>で</td><td></td><td>い</td></tr>
<tr><td>き</td><td>ま</td><td>し</td><td>た</td><td>。</td><td>あ</td><td>さ</td><td></td><td>じ</td><td>ゅ</td><td>う</td><td>じ</td><td></td><td>に</td><td></td><td>と</td><td>う</td><td>ち</td><td>ゃ</td><td>く</td><td></td></tr>
<tr><td>し</td><td>ま</td><td>し</td><td>た</td><td>。</td><td>じ</td><td>ゅ</td><td>う</td><td>に</td><td>じ</td><td>は</td><td>ん</td><td></td><td>ご</td><td>ろ</td><td></td><td>し</td><td>ょ</td><td>く</td><td>じ</td><td></td></tr>
<tr><td>を</td><td></td><td>し</td><td>て</td><td>、</td><td>そ</td><td>れ</td><td>か</td><td>ら</td><td></td><td>よ</td><td>る</td><td></td><td>し</td><td>ち</td><td>じ</td><td></td><td>ま</td><td>で</td><td></td><td>か</td></tr>
<tr><td>い</td><td>ぎ</td><td></td><td>が</td><td></td><td>あ</td><td>り</td><td>ま</td><td>し</td><td>た</td><td>。</td><td>つ</td><td>ぎ</td><td></td><td>の</td><td></td><td>あ</td><td>さ</td><td></td><td>と</td><td>う</td></tr>
<tr><td>き</td><td>ょ</td><td>う</td><td></td><td>へ</td><td></td><td>か</td><td>え</td><td>り</td><td>ま</td><td>し</td><td>た</td><td>。</td><td>ら</td><td>い</td><td>し</td><td>ゅ</td><td>う</td><td></td><td>ま</td><td>た</td></tr>
<tr><td>り</td><td>ょ</td><td>こ</td><td>う</td><td></td><td>を</td><td></td><td>し</td><td>ま</td><td>す</td><td>。</td><td></td><td></td><td></td><td></td><td></td><td></td><td></td><td></td><td></td><td></td></tr>
</table>

Rōmaji: _____

_____

_____

_____

_____

_____

_____

けんじ　「おなか　が　すいて　しにそう　で
す。」

あきお　「まさか。あさごはん　から　にじか
ん　しか　たって　いません　よ。」

けんじ　「じつ　は、けさ　じかん　が　なく
て　たべる　こと　が　できません
でした。」

あきお　「こまりました　ね。いま、ここ　に
、なにも　ありません。おかね　は
あります　か。」

けんじ　「ひゃくえん　しか　ない　です。」

あきお　「ちょっと　たりません　ね。おかね
を　かして　あげましょう　か。」

けんじ　「はい、おねがい　します。」

Rōmaji: _____

_____

_____

_____

_____

_____

_____

_____

_____

_____

_____

_____

_____

_____

_____

Katakana exercises

Writing words

READ each of the following words several times and ROMANIZE it on the first line below it. CHECK your work against Appendix C; then cover the original words and REWRITE them in *KATAKANA* on the second line below each. CHECK your *KATAKANA* against the original words.

ランチ (lunch)
_____
_____

レストラン (restaurant)
_____
_____

ホットケーキ (hotcakes)
_____
_____

チーズ (cheese)
_____
_____

ハム (ham)
_____
_____

アイス クリーム (ice cream)
_____
_____

ピッツァ (pizza)
_____
_____

ハムエッグ (ham & eggs)
_____
_____

アップル・パイ (apple pie)
_____
_____

コーヒー (coffee)
_____
_____

オムレツ (omelet)
_____
_____

ジュース (juice)
_____
_____

サラダ (salad)
_____
_____

パン (bread)
_____
_____

マヨネーズ (mayonnaise)
_____
_____

ドーナツ (donut)
_____
_____

ケチャップ (ketchup)
_____
_____

クリーム・ソーダ (cream soda)
_____
_____

デザート (dessert)
_____
_____

ソーセージ (sausage)
_____
_____

スパゲッティー (spaghetti)
_____
_____

チョコレート・ケーキ (chocolate cake)
_____
_____

オレンジ・ジュース (orange juice)
_____
_____

チーズバーガー (cheeseburger)
_____
_____

ハンバーガー (hamburger)
_____
_____

ポテト・フライ (french fries)
_____
_____

サンドイッチ (sandwich)
_____
_____

スプーン (spoon)
_____

フォーク (fork)
_____

ナイフ (knife)
_____

コップ (glass/tumbler)
_____

スポーツ (sports)
_____
_____

テニス (tennis)
_____
_____

バスケットボール (basketball)
_____
_____

ゴルフ (golf)
_____
_____

ボクシング (boxing)
_____
_____

フットボール (football)
_____
_____

サッカー (soccer)
_____
_____

スキー (skiing)
_____
_____

ピンポン (ping-pong)
_____
_____

ベイスボール (baseball)
_____
_____

スケート (skating)
_____
_____

プロ・レスリング (pro wrestling)
_____
_____

インターネット (Internet)
_____
_____

コンピューター (computer)
_____
_____

データ (data)
_____
_____

モニター (monitor)
_____
_____

パスワード (password)
_____
_____

ハード・ドライブ (hard drive)
_____
_____

ソフトウエア (software)
_____
_____

アプリ (app/application)
_____
_____

ウエブサイト (website)
_____
_____

サイト・マップ (site map)
_____
_____

ダウンロード (download)
_____
_____

パソコン (personal computer)
_____
_____

アメリカ (America)
_____
_____

アジア (Asia)
_____
_____

オーストラリア (Australia)
_____
_____

ヨーロッパ (Europe)
_____
_____

アフリカ (Africa)
_____
_____

ニューヨーク (New York)
_____
_____

イギリス (England)
_____
_____

フランス (France)
_____
_____

ロサンゼルス (Los Angeles)
_____
_____

イタリヤ (Italy)
_____
_____

ロシア (Russia)
_____
_____

パリ (Paris)
_____
_____

ハワイ (Hawaii)
_____
_____

ワイキキ (Waikiki)
_____
_____

アイランド (island)
_____
_____

ツアー (tour)
_____
_____

ショー (show)
_____
_____

ラスベガス (Las Vegas)
_____
_____

カジノ (casino)
_____
_____

ゲーム (game)
_____
_____

レンタカー (rental car)
_____
_____

ホテル (hotel)
_____
_____

ロビー (lobby)
_____
_____

ルーム・サービス (room service)
_____
_____

ボーイ (bellboy/waiter)
_____
_____

パスポート (passport)
_____
_____

ガソリン (gasoline)
_____
_____

バス (bus)
_____
_____

タクシー (taxi)
_____
_____

トラック (truck)
_____
_____

オートバイ (motorcycle)
_____
_____

ビジネス (business)
_____
_____

ショッピング (shopping)
_____
_____

セールスマン (salesman)
_____
_____

セール (sale)
_____
_____

デパート (department store)
_____
_____

クレジット・カード (credit card)
_____
_____

バーゲン (bargain)
_____
_____

エスカレーター (escalator)
_____
_____

セルフサービス (self-service)
_____
_____

ニュース (news)
_____
_____

テレビ (television)
_____
_____

ラジオ (radio)
_____
_____

テーブル (table)
_____
_____

アパート (apartment)
_____
_____

マンション (large apartment)
_____
_____

ベッド (bed)
_____
_____

トイレ (toilet)
_____
_____

スーツ (suit)
_____
_____

ズボン (trousers)
_____
_____

シャツ (shirt)
_____
_____

ワイシャツ (white shirt)
_____
_____

ドレス (dress)
_____
_____

パジャマ (pajamas)
_____
_____

ネクタイ (necktie)
_____
_____

ジーパン (jeans)
_____
_____

ブラウス (blouse)
_____
_____

スカート (skirt)
_____
_____

パンツ (underpants)
_____
_____

マスク (face mask)
_____
_____

アスピリン (aspirin)
_____
_____

ウイルス (virus)
_____
_____

インフルエンザ (flu, influenza)
_____
_____

アレルギー (allergy)
_____
_____

ボランティア (volunteer)
_____
_____

パート (part-time job)
_____
_____

アルバイト (extra job)
_____
_____

ジャケット (jacket)
_____
_____

スーパー (supermarket)
_____
_____

クリスマス (Christmas)
_____
_____

サンタ・クロース (Santa Claus)
_____
_____

キャンデー (candy)
_____
_____

ピアノ (piano)
_____
_____

ギター (guitar)
_____
_____

クレヨン (crayon)
_____
_____

ファッション (fashion)
_____
_____

モデル (model)
_____
_____

カメラ (camera)
_____
_____

ビデオ (video)
_____
_____

シーディー (CD)
_____
_____

Writing sentences and paragraphs

READ each sentence or paragraph several times, then ROMANIZE them on the lines below each. CHECK your romanization against the correct responses in Appendix C. Then cover the original sentence or paragraph and REWRITE it in *KANA* on a copy of the writing grid (pp. 129–130). CHECK your *KANA* sentence or paragraph against the original. (Translations of all sentences and paragraphs are in Appendix D.)

わたくし の アパート は せまくて くら
い です が、 ともだち の マンション は
ひろくて あかるい です。

Rōmaji: _____

_____

スポーツ が とても すき です。 ベイスボ
ール と サッカー が だいすき です。 テ
ニス も します が、 ゴルフ の ほう が
じょうず だ と おもいます。

Rōmaji: _____

_____

_____

スミス せんせい は クラス で いつも
ワイシャツ と ネクタイ を します。

Rōmaji: _____

となり の おにいさん は デパート で
はたらいて います が、 アルバイト を さ
がして いる そう です。

Rōmaji: _____

_____

せんしゅう あたらしい コンピューター を
かいました が、 モニター が こわれて い
た ので、 きのう かえしました。

Rōmaji: _____

_____

まいにち				おしごと			に		いく		とき、		バス	
で		いきますか、それとも									タクシー			で
いきますか。														

Rōmaji: _____

_____

_____

ちょっと				きぶん		が		わるい		です		が、	ウ	
イ	ル	ス		か		アレルギー				か		わかりません。		

Rōmaji: _____

ヨーロッパ					に		いった		とき		、	おおきい		ホ
テ	ル	に		とまりました。					ロビー			だけ		で
う	ち	の		アパート			より		おおきい			です。		

Rōmaji: _____

_____

ア	ン	ダ	ー	ソ	ン	さ	ん		は		まいしゅう			にちよう
び		に		びょういん				で		ボランティア				を
し	ま	す	。											

Rōmaji: _____

レ	ス	ト	ラ	ン		の		まえ		に		たって		いる	ひ
と		は		ジョンソン				せんせい			の		ともだち	
で	は		ありません				か	。						

Rōmaji: _____

_____

_____

ま	い	し	ゅ	う			げ	つ	よ	う	び		に
ち	か	く		の			レ						

まいしゅう　げつようび　に　ちかく　の　レストラン　で　あさごはん　を　たべます。いつも　ホットケーキ　と　オレンジ・ジュース　を　ちゅうもん　します。でも、あした　は　したぶん　ソーセージ　か　ハムエッグ　に　しよう　と　おもいます。コーヒー　は　のみません　が、ジュース　が　だいすき　です。

Rōmaji: _____

_____

きょねん　かぞく　と　アメリカ　へ　いってきました。ひこうき　で　ハワイ　に　いって、ホノルル　に　みっかかん　とまりました。アイランド・ツアー　を　して、つぎ　の　ひ、ワイキキ・ビーチ　で　あそびました。それから　ロサンゼルス　を　けいゆ　して、ラスベガス　へ　いきました。そこ　の　グランド・ホテル　に　とまって、バス　で　ツアー　を　して、よる　は　カジノ　と　ショー　を　たのしみました。

Rōmaji: _____

_____

_____

さくばん　ゆうしょく　を　たべて、テレビ
の　ニュース　を　みました。それから　こど
も　を　つれて　アイスクリーム　を　たべ
に　いきました。うち　に　かえって　ビデオ
・ゲーム　を　したり、ほん　を　よんだり
しました。こども　が　ねた　あと、じゅうに
じ　まで　テレビ　で　プロ・レスリング　を
みました。

Rōmaji: _____

_____

_____

_____

_____

_____

_____

_____

この　しゃしん　は　きょねん　の　クリスマ
ス　の　とき　デパート　で　とりました。こ
ども　を　つれて　サンタ・クロース　を　み
に　いきました。この　べつ　の　しゃしん
は　おなじ　ひ　です　が、ともだち　の　む
すめ　です。かのじょ　は　ファッション・モ
デル　です　よ。とても　きれい　な　ひと
です　ね。おかあさん　と　ふたり　で　とな
り　の　マンション　に　すんで　います。

Rōmaji: _____

_____

_____

_____

_____

_____

_____

き	ん	よ	う	び		は		わ	た	し		の		た	ん	じ	ょ	う	び	
で	し	た	。	お	か	あ	さ	ん		は		チ	ョ	コ	レ	ー	ト	・	ケ	ー
キ		を		つ	く	っ	て		く	れ	ま	し	た	。	お	じ	い	さ	ん	
と		お	ば	あ	さ	ん		に		お	か	ね		を		も	ら	っ	て	、
あ	た	ら	し	い		ジ	ー	パ	ン		と		サ	ン	ダ	ル		を		か
い	ま	し	た	。	ラ	ン	チ		が		お	わ	っ	て		か	ら	、	こ	う
え	ん		に		い	っ	て	、	ス	ケ	ー	ト		を		し	ま	し	た	。
と	て	も		い	い		バ	ー	ス	デ	イ		で	し	た	。				

Rōmaji: _____

_____

_____

_____

_____

_____

あ	べ		「	ケ	ン	さ	ん	、	し	ゃ	ち	ょ	う		が		き	ょ	う	
			ラ	ン	チ		を		ご	ち	そ	う		し	て		く	れ	ま	す
			が	、	な	に		が		い	い		で	す		か	。	ピ	ッ	ツ
			ァ		か		ハ	ン	バ	ー	ガ	ー		か	、	ど	ち	ら		が
			い	い		で	す		か	。	」									
ケ	ン		「	チ	ー	ズ	バ	ー	ガ	ー		が		い	い		で	す		ね
			。	そ	し	て		ポ	テ	ト	・	フ	ラ	イ		も		お	ね	が
			い		で	き	ま	す		か	。	」								
あ	べ		「	の	み	も	の		は		い	か	が		で	す		か	。	」
ケ	ン		「	ソ	ー	ダ		が		い	い		で	す		ね	。	」		

Rōmaji: _____

_____

_____

_____

_____

_____

_____

うちのしゅじんはイギリスじんで、えいごもフランスごもイタリヤごもはなします。わたしはにほんでうまれましたが、にさいからフランスにすんでいて、フランスごのほうがじょうずです。いもうとはフランスでうまれましたけれども、ロシアじんとけっこんしました。あのひとはロシアごもフランスごもよくわかります。

Rōmaji: _____

デパートでバーゲン・セールをしていましたから、けさはやくそこにいきました。こどもにパジャマとパンツをかって、わたしにはブラウスとスカートをかいました。しゅじんはスーツが、ひつようですが、ズボンとワイシャツとネクタイしかかいませんでした。

Rōmaji: _____

Katakana-only exercise

READ the following paragraph several times, then ROMANIZE it on the lines below. CHECK your work against the correct responses in Appendix C. Then cover the original and REWRITE the romanized paragraph on a copy of the writing grid (pp. 129–130) in *KATAKANA* only. CHECK your *KATAKANA* against the original paragraph. (See Appendix D for a translation of the paragraph.)

セ	ン	シ	ュ	ウ		ガ	ッ	コ	ウ		ガ		ハ	ジ	マ	リ	マ	シ	タ	。 ト
ナ	リ		ノ		ト	モ	ダ	チ		ハ		ボ	ク		ト		オ	ナ	ジ	レ
キ	シ		ノ		ク	ラ	ス		ヲ		ト	ッ	テ		イ	マ	ス		カ	ラ、
イ	ッ	シ	ョ		ニ		ベ	ン	キ	ョ	ウ		シ	マ	ス	。 ク	ラ	ス		ガ
オ	ワ	ッ	テ		カ	ラ		ス	グ		ト	シ	ョ	カ	ン		ヘ		イ	ッ テ
、	キ	ョ	ウ	カ	シ	ョ		ヲ		ヨ	ン	デ	、	シ	ュ	ク	ダ	イ		ヲ
シ	マ	ス	。 ア	ト	デ		シ	ョ	ク	ド	ウ		デ		ラ	ン	チ			ヲ
タ	ベ	マ	ス	。 イ	チ	ジ		ニ		ト	モ	ダ	チ		ハ		エ	イ	ゴ	
ノ		ク	ラ	ス		ヘ		イ	ッ	テ	、	ボ	ク		ハ		サ	ン	ジ	マ
デ		ク	ラ	ス		ガ		ナ	イ		ノ	デ	、	ヒ	ト	リ		デ		ト シ
ョ	カ	ン		ニ		モ	ド	ッ	テ	、	ベ	ン	キ	ョ	ウ		ヲ		ツ	ズ ケ
マ	ス	。 ス	ウ	ガ	ク		ノ		ク	ラ	ス		ガ		オ	ワ	ッ	テ	、	ウ
チ		ヘ		カ	エ	リ	マ	ス	。											

Rōmaji: _____

_____

_____

_____

_____

_____

_____

_____

Writing practice grid

On the next page is a writing grid that you should find helpful in improving your handwriting as you practice. This grid can be used for both horizontal and vertical writing practice.

You can make copies of the writing practice grid on the next page, or to access the online writing practice grid for this book, please follow these instructions:

1. Go to mhprofessional.com/mediacenter.

2. Enter this book's ISBN: 978-0-07-182798-0 and select the Find Product button.

3. Enter your e-mail address to receive a link to the downloadable files.

You can then save and print copies of the writing practice grid for your handwriting practice.

Machine-made characters

(cf. pp. 3–28 and 59–80)

Hiragana

GOJŪON

あいうえお
かきくけこ
さしすせそ
たちつてと
なにぬねの
はひふへほ
まみむめも
や　ゆ　よ
らりるれろ
わ　　　を
ん

VOICED & BILABIALIZED

がぎぐげご
ざじずぜぞ
だぢづでど
ばびぶべぼ
ぱぴぷぺぽ

COMBINATION CHARACTERS

きゃ ぎゃ しゃ じゃ ちゃ ぢゃ にゃ ひゃ びゃ ぴゃ みゃ りゃ
きゅ ぎゅ しゅ じゅ ちゅ ぢゅ にゅ ひゅ びゅ ぴゅ みゅ りゅ
きょ ぎょ しょ じょ ちょ ぢょ にょ ひょ びょ ぴょ みょ りょ

Katakana

ワ	ラ リ ル レ ロ	ヤ ユ ヨ	マ ミ ム メ モ	ハ ヒ フ ヘ ホ	ナ ニ ヌ ネ ノ	タ チ ツ テ ト	サ シ ス セ ソ	カ キ ク ケ コ	ア イ ウ エ オ
ヲ ン									

VOICED & BILABIALIZED

パ ピ プ ペ ポ	バ ビ ブ ベ ボ	ダ ヂ ヅ デ ド	ザ ジ ズ ゼ ゾ	ガ ギ グ ゲ ゴ

COMBINATION CHARACTERS

リャ	ミャ	ピャ	ビャ	ヒャ	ニャ	ヂャ	チャ	ジャ	シャ	ギャ	キャ
リュ	ミュ	ピュ	ビュ	ヒュ	ニュ	ヂュ	チュ	ジュ	シュ	ギュ	キュ
リョ	ミョ	ピョ	ビョ	ヒョ	ニョ	ヂョ	チョ	ジョ	ショ	ギョ	キョ

APPENDIX B

Exceptions in Kana

1. EXCEPTIONAL LONG "O" *(cf. pp. 31–32)*

In some words the vowel sound /O/ is elongated by the character お *(O)* rather than う *(U)*.

For your information, these exceptional words were anciently written with *HO* (ほ) as the second *O*; for example, おおい *(ŌI)* was once written おほい *(OHOI)*. Since it is impossible to tell from the word itself whether it falls into this category or not, it is necessary to memorize the exceptions. There are only a few, the most common of which are listed here.

HŌ ほお	*KŌRI* こおり	*TŌ* とお	*ŌU* おおう
"cheek"	"ice"	"ten"	"to cover"

TŌI とおい	*TŌRI / DŌRI* とおり どおり	*TŌRU* とおる
"far away"	"street," "road," "highway"	"to pass through"

Also, any time the word begins with the prefix *Ō*, meaning "big," this exception applies.

ŌKII おおきい	*ŌSAKA* おおさか
"big"	the city "Osaka"

ŌKAMI おおかみ	*ŌHASHI* おおはし
"wolf"	"big bridge"

2. EXCEPTIONAL *JI* AND *ZU* *(cf. p. 16, notes 2 and 3)*

The voiced characters ぢ *(JI)* and づ *(ZU)* are used only occasionally and in the following instances:

A. when the word originally used the character ち or つ but became voiced when combined with another word to make a compound, such as:

KOZUTSUMI こづつみ   *(TSUTSUMI* = "package"; *KO* = "small")
"postal package"

HANAJI はなぢ   *(CHI* = "blood"; *HANA* = "nose")
"nosebleed"

Note: the word *ICHINICHIJŪ*, which is a compound of *ICHINICHI* ("one day") and *CHŪ* ("center") and means "all day long," is written in this book with ぢゅ, according to rule A above. However, current common usage leans toward writing this word with じゅ: いちにちじゅう

continued

B. when the voiced character is a repetition of its unvoiced counterpart, as in:

CHIJIMU　　ちぢむ
"to shrink"

TSUZUKU　　つづく
"to continue"

APPENDIX C

Answers to practice exercises and self-tests

PAGE 40
1. Kore wa nan desu ka?   2. Sore wa tokei desu.   3. Ano hito wa dare desu ka?   4. Kanojo wa tanaka-san desu.   5. Shokudō wa asoko desu ka?   6. O-tearai wa doko desu ka?   7. Kare wa sensei dewa arimasen.   8. Ano hito wa gaijin desu ka?   9. Yūbinkyoku wa mukō desu.
10. Watakushi wa gakusei deshita.   11. Iriguchi wa asoko desu, ne?

PAGE 41
1. Nan desu ka?   2. Toshokan wa doko ni arimasu ka?   3. Ginkō wa mukō ni arimasu.   4. Jūgyōin wa doko ni imasu ka?   5. Jūgyōin wa ano heya ni imasu.   6. Ano heya ni wa gomibako ga arimasu ka?   7. Kyōshitsu ni tsukue ga arimasen.   8. Ano heya ni dare ga imashita ka?   9. Kare wa imasen.

PAGE 42
1. Yoku irasshaimashita.   2. Doko e ikimasu ka?   3. Kesa gakkō ni kimashita.   4. Kinō tanaka-san wa jimusho ni kimasen deshita.   5. Shachō-san wa kyō takushii de kaerimashita.   6. Anata wa mō kaerimasu ka?   7. Kanojo wa nan de tōkyō ni ikimashita ka?   8. Watakushi wa kinō yūbinkyoku e ikimasen deshita.   9. Kare wa tomodachi desu.

PAGE 43
1. Ano hito wa nihongo o benkyō shite imasu ka?   2. Shachō-san ni mō ichido denwa o shite kudasai.   3. Kanojo wa shinbun o yonde imasen.   4. Tanaka-san wa kuruma o yūbinkyoku made unten shimashita.   5. Watakushi wa hon'ya e ikimashita keredomo, hon o kaimasen deshita.
6. Kyō watakushi to tabete kudasaimasen ka?

PAGE 44
1. Anata wa naze kyōshitsu ni ikimasen ka?   2. Ashita made denwa shinaide kudasai.   3. Raishū mata kuru koto ga dekimasu ka?   4. Konban isogashii desu kara, iku koto ga dekimasen.
5. O-kyaku-sama ga sugu kimasu node, mada kaeranaide kudasai.   6. Oniisan wa naze tabemasen deshita ka?   7. Jūichiji made benkyō shimashō, ne?

PAGE 45
1. Dō iu imi desu ka?   2. Shitsumon ga arimasu ka?   3. Ohayō gozaimasu.   4. Oyasumi nasai.
5. Aa , sō desu ka?   6. Dewa mata.   7. Wakarimasu, deshō?   8. Sayōnara.   9. Ikura desu ka?
10. Ichimangosen-nihyakujū-doru desu.   11. Takai desu, ne?   12. Iie, yasui desu yo.   13. O-namae wa nan desu ka?   14. Tanaka to mōshimasu.   15. Hajimemashite.   16. Yoroshiku o-negai shimasu.
17. Dōmo arigatō gozaimasu.   18 . Dō itashimashite.   19. Kyū-hyakurokujūgoen desu.

PAGE 46
1. Deguchi wa doko desu ka?   2. Iriguchi wa mukō desu, ne?   3. Kare wa sensei dewa arimasen ka?
4. Watakushi no daigaku wa tōkyō ni arimasu.   5. Anata no tsukue wa dore desu ka?   6. Zannen desu, ne?   7. Jimusho ni wa gomibako mo tokei mo arimasu.   8. Dono heya ga kare no desu ka?
9. Kyōshitsu ni wa, sensei mo gakusei mo imasu.   10. Shachō-san to jūgyōin wa ima sono heya ni imasu ka?   11. Anata no kuruma wa mukō ni arimasen deshita.

PAGE 47

1. Irasshaimase.   2. Kondo wa issho ni ikimashō   3. Senshū yūbinkyoku e ikimashita ka?   4. Raishū mainichi onēsan to issho ni chikatetsu de kaerimasu.   5. Go-chisō-sama deshita.   6. Chotto matte kudasai.   7. Itte kimasu. 8. Okāsan to onēsan wa issho ni shokudō de tabete imashita.   9. Kare wa jūji jūgofun mae ni kaerimashita. 10. Sakuban daigaku no deguchi de tanaka-san to matte imashita.   11. Otōto wa ōsaka de hataraite imasu ka? 12. Imōto wa ima heya de tegami o yonde imasu.

PAGE 48

1. O-jama shimasu.   2. O-tanjōbi ōmedetō gozaimasu.   3. Itsumo doko de kyūkei o shimasu ka?   4. Ichinichijū benkyō suru koto ga dekimasen deshita.   5. Okane ga arimasen node, mada hon o kawanaide kudasai.   6 . Minna wa nihongo ga dekimasu ka?   7. Otōsan wa kotoshi nihon de ryokō o shite imasu.   8. Ashita no asa, gakkō de sensei to hanashite kudasaimasen ka?   9. O-naka ga suite imasu keredomo, mada shokuji ga dekimasen.   10. Getsuyōbi wa kyūjitsu desu kara, watakushi-tachi wa shigoto e ikimasen.

PAGE 49

Tanaka: "Sensei wa kyōshitsu ni imasu ka?"
Honda: "Iie, jimusho ni imasu."
Tanaka: "Jimusho wa doko ni arimasu ka?"
Honda: "Mukō ni arimasu."
Tanaka: "Kono hen ni wa gomibako ga arimasu ka?"
Honda: "Gomibako wa ano heya ni arimasu."
Tanaka: "O-tearai mo arimasu ka?"
Honda: "Iie, arimasen. Toshokan ni arimasu."
Tanaka: "Dōmo arigatō gozaimasu."

PAGE 50

Satō: "O-tomodachi ni denwa o shimashō ka?"
Aki: "Kyō imasen kara, mada shinaide kudasai."
Satō: "Hai, wakarimashita. Dewa, toshokan e ikimashō ka?"
Aki: "Sumimasen ga, kyō isoide imasu node, dekimasen. Gomen nasai, ne?"
Satō: "Ii desu yo. Ashita wa dō desu ka?"
Aki: "Hai, ashita wa kekkō desu yo."

PAGE 51

1. それ は あなた の ほんです か。   2. かれ は せんせい では ありません でした。 3. としょかん は むこう です。   4. あなた は がくせい では ありません か。 5. ゆうびんきょく は どれ です か。   6. それ は かのじょ の じしょ です、ね。 7. あの ひと の つくえ は あそこ です。   8. たなかさん の とけい は たかい、でしょう。   9. あの ひとびと は だいがくせい でした。   10. むこう の ひと は しゃちょうさん です、ね。   11. ほんやさん は がいじん です。   12. わたくしたち は にほんじん では ありません。

PAGE 52

1. おともだち は いま しょくどう に います。   2. おてあらい は どこ に あります か。   3. わたくし は くるま が ありません。   4. かのじょ は せんしゅう とうきょう に いました。   5. せいとたち は きのう きょうしつ に いません でした。   6. あの へや に は だれ が います か。   7. この じてんしゃ は かれ の では ありません。 8. じゅうぎょういん も しゃちょうさん も じむしょ に います。 9. ごみばこ も おてあらい に あります か。   10. あの ひとびと は きのう の あさ ゆうびんきょく に いました。   11. しょくどう は あそこ に あります、ね。   12. ぎんこう も としょかん も そこ に あります。

1. あなた は きょう としょかん に いきます か。　2. ゆうべ しょくどう へ いきません でした。　3. しゃちょうさん は ひこうき で とうきょう へ いきました、でしょう。　4. おねえさん は まいにち ちかてつ で かえります。　5. せんげつ みんな は でんしゃ で きました。　6. らいねん ふね で いきましょう。　7. おにいさん と いっしょ に きました、ね。　8. いま わたくし は じかん が ありません。　9. いもうとさん は もう かえりました か。　10. おともだち は ひこうき で ちゅうごく へ かえりましたか。　11. ごしゅじん は さくばん の かい に いきました か。　12. たなか さん は あした さっぽろ へ かえります。

1. あなた は いま なに を して います か.　2. かれ の りょうしん は おおさか に すんで います。　3. かのじょ は へや で てがみ を かいて います。　4. おにいさん と おとうさん は いっしょ に はしって いました。　5. おともだち と むこう に すわって ください。　6. みんな は もう うち へ かえって います。　7. すこし べんきょう して くださいません か。　8. としょかん へ いきます けれども、べんきょう しません。　9. たなかさん は けさ むこう に たって いました。　10. かのじょたち は まだ きゅうけい を して います。　11. あの うた を うたって くださいます か。　12. わたくし は ぎんこう で はたらいて いません でした。

1. あした は きゅうじつ です から、やすんで ください。　2. にほんご を はなす こと が できます か。　3. びょうき です ので、じむしょ へ いかないで ください。　4. らいげつ の かい に いく こと が できません か。　5. かのじょ は うたう こと が できません。　6. もう すこし まつ こと が できます か。　7. たかい です ので、かわないで ください。　8. あなた は なぜ はんかがい へ いきません でした か。　9. じかん が ありません から、まだ たべないで ください。　10. きょうしつ で ともだち と はなさないで ください。　11. くるま が ありません から、でんしゃ で いきます。　12. えいご が できません ので、にほんご で はなして いました。

1. David　2. Raymond　3. Carolyn　4. Shirley　5. Smith　6. Johnson　7. Anderson　8. Thompson　9. Roberts 10. White　11. Carter　12. Lampkin

1. Tanaka-san wa dono yō na hito desu ka?　2. Watakushi wa chiisai apāto ni sunde imasu.　3. Shachō-san wa suteki na hito desu, ne?　4. Sakuban no kai wa osokatta desu ka?　5. Kono daigaku ni wa dono yō na hito ga imasu ka?

1. Tanaka-san wa kesa nanji ni kimashita ka?　2. Watakushi wa shachō-san ga hawai ni iku to omoimasu.　3. Kare ga hachiji made matsu to omoimasen.　4. Mō denwa o shita to omoimasu.　5. Okāsan wa mada kaimono o shimasen deshita.

1. Watakushi wa hankagai ni itte, kaimono o shimashita.　2. Hawai ni iku toki, tomodachi no uchi ni tomarimasu. 3. Eiga o miru koto ga suki desu.　4. Okāsan wa soko ni itte kaerimashita.　5. Kyanpu o suru koto wa tanoshii to omoimasu.

1. Mukō ni suwatte iru hito wa dare desu ka?   2. Konban eiga ni ikitai to omoimasu.   3. Watakushi wa tomodachi to benkyō shitai to omoimasu.   4. Kyōshitsu de hanashita hito wa dare deshita ka?   5. Kinō nanimo shitakunakatta desu.

1. Chotto hanashite mo ii desu ka?   2. Ashita made denwa shinakute mo ii desu ka?   3. Hon'ya de tabete wa ikemasen.   4. Shachō-san to hanasanakute wa ikemasen.   5. Mainichi kusuri o nomanakute wa dame desu. 6. Mo kaette mo ii desu.

1. Anata no kuruma wa ōkii desu ka?   2. Kinō no tesuto wa muzukashikatta desu.   3. Kyō wa sugoku samui desu. 4. Kanojo no onēsan wa utsukushi desu keredomo, amari yasashikunai desu, ne?   5 . Tanaka-san wa genki na hito desu.   6. Dō iu apāto ni sunde imasu ka?   7. Benri desu ga, amari yasukunai desu.   8. Kanojo wa kesa byōki ni narimashita.   9. Otōsan wa kare ga suki desu node, kanemochi ni shimashita.   10. Shigoto wa takusan arimashita kara, osokunarimashita.   11. Ano kodomo wa hijō ni kashikoi desu.

1. Orenjiiro no hana mo kiiro no hana mo arimasu.   2. Narau yori, nare yo.   3. Kanojo wa ringo ga suki da to iimashita.   4. Okane ga nai kara, kaimono ga dekimasen.   5. Kore wa toshokan dewanai to omoimasu.   6. Kanojo wa nihon ni itta to iimashita.   7. Tōkyō no depāto e ikimashita ga, nanimo kaimasen deshita.   8. Karera ga tomodachi to tabete inakatta to iimashita.   9. Kare no nihongo wa amari jōzu dewanai to omoimasu.   10. Kyō anata wa nani o shimashita ka?   11. Kesa gohan o tabete, gakkō e ikimashita.

1. Nihonshoku o tabetakunakatta kara, tomodachi to shokudō e ikimasen deshita.   2. Anata wa nanji ni tabetai to omoimasu ka?   3. Yoji made ni denwa o shinakute wa ikenai to omoimasu.   4. Mō denwa o shite mo ii desu ka? 5. Yoku ganbaranakute wa dame desu yo.   6. Koko de tabako o nonde mo ii to omoimasu ka?   7. Nanimo shinakute mo ii desu ka?   8. Otomodachi ga unten shite wa dame desu.   9. Otōsan ga konakute wa ikemasen.   10. Kyō mo ashita mo benkyō shinakute wa ikemasen.

1. Fuyu ni natte, sukii o shimashita.   2. Ano hito wa nihonjin de eigo ga dekimasen.   3. Karera wa isshōkenmei ni hataraite imasu.   4. Shachō-san wa hijō ni taisetsu na yōji ga aru to iimashita.   5. Kanojo wa hontō ni kirei desu. 6. Konban watakushi wa eiga ni ikitai to omoimasu ga issho ni itte kudasaimasen ka?   7. Tanoshimi ni shite imasu.   8. Yūbinkyoku de hataraite iru kirei na onna no hito wa dare desu ka?   9. Watakushi wa kyō nanimo shitakunai to omoimasu.

1. Aisu-kuriimu o tabemashō ka?   2. Kinō no tesuto wa muzukashikatta desu, ne!   3. Kono apāto wa amari benri dewa arimasen.   4. Apāto o kirei ni shite kudasai.   5. Orenjiiro no kuruma wa watakushi no desu.   6. Amerika-jin wa itsumo sandoitchi o taberu to iimashita.   7. Kare wa san furanshisuko e ikimashita keredomo, rosu e ikimasen deshita.   8. Terebi o mite ita toki, poppukōn o tabemashita.

1. Oniisan wa nyū yōku ni sunde imasu ga, furansu de benkyō shimashita.   2. Yama made hitchihaiku o shite, kyanpu o shimashita.   3. Hawai e iku toki, honoruru no hoteru ni tomarimasu.   4. Howaitosan wa supeinjin no otomodachi ga raishū kuru to iimashita.   5. Ima L.A. Times (taimuzu) o yonde iru hito wa sumisu-san desu. 6. Shiroi sētā o kite iru hawaijin wa "sutā uōzu" to iu eiga o mite kimashita.

PAGE 99

1. タナカサン ハ ゲンキ ナ ヒト デス、ネ。 2. ドウ イウ アパート ニ スンデ イマス カ。 3. ベンリ デス ガ、アマリ オオキクナイ デス。 4. キョウ ハ ハヤク アツクナリマシタ。 5. ムコウ ノ オトコ ノ ヒト ハ イッショウケンメイ ニ ハタライテ イマス。 6. カイ ハ ゼンゼン オモシロクナカッタ デス ヨ。 7. アナタ ハ ニホンショク ガ スキ デス カ。 8. イチバン スキ ナ イロ ハ ナニイロ デス カ。 9. オニイサン ハ キノウ ウチ ニ カエッタ トキ、ナニ ヲ シマシタ カ。 10. ブチョウサン ガ アタラシイ クルマ ヲ カッタ ト イイマシタ。 11. カノジョ ハ ウタウ コト ガ デキル ト オモイマセン。 12. カレ ノ クルマ ガ アカイ ト イッタ ト オモイマス。

PAGE 100

1. カレ ハ キョウ シゴト ニ イカナカッタ デス。 2. アノ ヒト ハ ジムショ ニ コナカッタ ト オモイマス。 3. サクバン ノ カイ ハ ナガクナクテ ヨカッタ デス。 4. アノ ホン ハ ベツ ニ オモシロクナイ デス。 5. ドヨウビ ワタクシ ハ オジイサン ノ トコロ ヘ イキマシタ。 6. カノジョ ハ マイニチ ダイガク デ ハタラキマス。 7. アナタ ハ ナニ ガ ホシイ ト オモイマス カ。 8. エンピツ ガ ヒツヨウ ダ ト イイマシタ。 9. アノ ヒト ハ エキ ヲ サガシテ イル ト イイマシタ。 10. ホンヤ ヘ イッテ、オカアサン ノ タノンダ ホン ヲ カイマシタ。 11. モウ カエッテ モ イイ デス カ。 12. ゲツヨウビ ニ マタ ガッコウ ヘ イカナケレバナリマセン。

PAGE 101

1. スミス せんせい の おねえさん は ハワイ に すんで います。 2. わたくし の カメラ は だめ に なりました。 3. まずい ハンバーガー を たべました ので、びょうき に なりました。 4. オレンジいろ の セーター を きている ひと は おともだち です か。 5. かれ は アメリカ の ぎんこう で はたらいて います。 6. あした デパート へ いって、ミッキー マウス の とけい を かいます。 7. ともだち は フランス の だいがく で べんきょう して います。 8. ランチ が おわって、スーパー に いきたい と おもいます。 9. おかあさん は バス で はんかがい へ いきました。 10. ステーキ と サラダ を ちゅうもん しました か. 11. ここ で タバコ を のんでも いい です か。 12. えいがかん に いって、「シンデレラ」と いう えいが を みました。

PAGE 102

1. あの ペン は じゅうドル よんじゅうごセント で たかい です。 2. かれ は スエーデンじん で、フランスご と ドイツご を はなします。 3. いま スキー を して いない ひと は びょうき です か。 4. アイスクリーム が だいすき で、まいにち たべます。 5. スナック へ いって、サンドイッチ を たべましょう か。 6. タクシー で いって きました か。 7. セール が あった から、おかあさん は スーパー に いきました。 8. ガソリン が ない から、くるま を うんてん できません。 9. なんページ まで よみました か? 10. ラジオ を きいて いる ひと は メキシコじん だ と おもいます。 11. スミスさん と ブラウンさん は ヨーロッパ で りょこう を して います。 12. ホテル の レストラン で しょくじ を しました。

PAGE 107

- aeru • aozora • aisatsu
- enpitsu • eien • ehon
- idai • noberu • usui
- oriru • ueru • keiken
- oishii • sagasu • sensei
- kokuseki • gomi • kokoro
- ginkō • kikai • gunjin
- genki • shitsurei • gaikoku

PAGE 108

- gimon • isogu • jisho • kongetsu
- tsunami • zutsū • chikatetsu • senshū
- namae • doku • netsu • sokutatsu
- zasshi • okurimono • dame • zenzen
- tōchaku • kanazuchi • tetsudai • chijimeru
- dekakeru • nusumu • nomimono • tokidoki
- hairu • himitsu • hebi • nichiyōbi
- obake • batsu • ōi • futsū
- binbō • zenbu • wanpaku • honbu
- benri • kappatsu • pittari • junbi
- kippu • teppen • bentō • bunpō
- boku • marui • michi • geppu
- pokkuri • musubu • megumi • konpon

PAGE 109

- mendō • mura • omosa • yakimeshi
- mohan • kanmuri • yachin • yakudatsu
- yasui • ōya • yuki • yureru
- sayū • yoake • kari • yōshoku
- karada • heiwa • akarui • rainen
- rippa • rekishi • hareru • rusu
- danro • wakai • gyaku • rōjin
- ryokō • kyōmi • gyūniku • zannen
- myōji • byōki • chōdo • kyūjitsu
- chairo • shashin • kyaku
- gyūnyū • ryōshin • nyūgaku
- chūshoku • gyosen • ryaku
- nyūjō • ryōri • ryūgaku

PAGE 110

- Kesa ame ga yoku futte imashita ga, jūniji goro ni harete, ima wa dokomo aozora desu.
- Kinō gakkō ga owatte kara tomodachi no uchi e itte, yūshoku o gochisō ni narimashita.
- Ashita wa kyūjitsu desu kara, dokoka e ikimashō ka.
- Zasshi mo shinbun mo arimasu ga, dochira o yomitai desu ka.
- Shinjuku eki wa hito ga ippai desu kara, totemo nigiyaka desu.

PAGE 111

- Haruyasumi ni densha de ryokō shita koto o nikki ni kakimashita.
- Hachigatsu no jūichinichi kara kaisha ga yokkakan yasumi ni narimasu node, Okinawa e ikitai desu.
- Raigetsu gakkō no shiken ga hajimarimasu node, korekara zutto benkyō shinakereba narimasen.
- Shōgakkō no mae de akai bōshi o kabutta onna no hito wa kodomo o matte imashita.
- Okāsan ni tegami o kakitai keredomo, enpitsu ga arimasen node, kashite kudasaimasu ka.
- Kensan wa hako no naka o sagasu to, futatsu no ōkii jagaimo to ninjin o ippon mitsukemashita.

PAGE 112

• Nihon no shiki wa haru to natsu to aki to fuyu desu. Haru wa ame ga yoku futte, hana ga sakimasu. Natsu wa atsui desu kara, hito wa umi e yoku dekakemasu. Aki ga kuru to, ki no ha wa kōyō shimasu. Sorekara samukunari, yuki ga furimasu. Ichiban suki na kisetsu wa dore desu ka.

• Watashitachi no niwa no mannaka ni, ōkii yukidaruma ga arimasu. Oniisan to watashi ga tsukutta mono desu. Watashi wa furui bōshi o yukidaruma no atama ni okimashita. Oniisan ga kitta ki no eda wa yukidaruma no ude ni narimashita. Okāsan wa shashin o totte kuremashita.

PAGE 113

• Chichi wa daiku de, kanazuchi ya nokogiri o yoku tsukaimasu. Haha wa kōtōgakkō de sūgaku o oshiete imasu. Ane wa kangofu de, byōin de hataraite imasu. Ani wa daigakusei de, shōrai ginkō no jūyaku ni naritai desu. Boku wa kyūkyūsha no untenshu ni naritai to omoimasu.

• Dōbutsuen ni itta koto ga arimasu ka. Iroiro na dōbutsu ga ite, omoshiroi tokoro desu. Tora mo kuma mo ite, zō ya kirin mo chiisai tori mo, hebi mo imasu. Watashi no ichiban suki na dōbutsu wa shimauma desu. Raishū kazoku to issho ni higashiyama dōbutsuen ni ikimasu.

PAGE 114

• Kinyōbi ni otōsan wa, "Ashita kōen ni ikō ka" to iimashita. Minna "Hai, ikō yo" to sakebimashita. Tsugi no asa, minna de densha ni notte yama no kōen e dekakemashita. Yama no shita kara nagai kaidan ga ue made tsuzukimasu. Ichijikan nobotte, yatto chōjō ni tōchaku shimashita.

• Uchi no chikaku ni hiroi kawa ga arimasu. Kawa no soba ni wa ahiru ga imasu. Oya wa niwa de, kodomo wa gowa imasu. Maishū nichiyōbi ni uchi no onēsan to ahiru no kazoku o mi ni ikimasu. Ijimemasen kara, ahiru wa kowagari-masen. Kondo no nichiyōbi, tabemono o motte ikimasu.

PAGE 115

• Kinō ojiisan no uchi e ikimashita. Ojiisan wa chotto toshi o totte imasu ga, totemo tanoshii hito da to omoimasu. Sugoku furui kuruma o motte imasu. Ojiisan to obāsan wa tabitabi kuruma de dokoka e asobi ni ikimasu. Kinō sannin de tonari no machi ni kuruma de itte kimashita.

• Senshū Ōsaka e hikōki de ikimashita. Asa jūji ni tōchaku shimashita. Jūnijihan goro shokuji o shite, sorekara yoru shichiji made kaigi ga arimashita. Tsugi no asa Tōkyō e kaerimashita. Raishū mata ryokō o shimasu.

PAGE 116

Kenji:	"Onaka ga suite shinisō desu."
Akio:	"Masaka. Asagohan kara nijikan shika tatte imasen yo."
Kenji:	"Jitsu wa, kesa jikan ga nakute taberu koto ga dekimasen deshita."
Akio:	"Komarimashita ne. Ima, koko ni, nanimo arimasen. Okane wa arimasu ka."
Kenji:	"Hyakuen shika nai desu."
Akio:	"Chotto tarimasen ne. Okane o kashite agemashō ka."
Kenji:	"Hai, onegai shimasu."

PAGE 117

• ranchi • resutoran • hottokēki
• chiizu • hamu • aisukuriimu
• pittsa • hamueggu • appuru pai
• kōhii • omuretsu • jūsu
• sarada • pan • mayonēzu
• dōnatsu • kechappu • kuriimu sōda
• dezāto • sōsēji • supagettii

PAGE 118

• chokorēto kēki • orenji jūsu
• chiizubāgā • hanbāgā
• poteto furai • sandoitchi
• supūn • fuōku • naifu • koppu
• supōtsu • tenisu • basukettobōru
• gorufu • bokushingu • futtobōru
• sakkā • sukii • pinpon
• beisubōru • sukēto • puro resuringu
• intānetto • konpyūtā • dēta
• monitā • pasuwādo • hādo doraibu
• sofutouea • apuri • uebusaito
• saito mappu • daunrōdo • pasokon

PAGE 119

- amerika • ajia • ōsutoraria
- yōroppa • afurika • nyūyōku
- igirisu • furansu • rosanzerusu
- itariya • roshia • pari
- hawai • waikiki • airando
- tsuā • shō • rasubegasu
- kajino • gēmu • rentakā
- hoteru • robii • rūmu sābisu
- bōi • pasupōto • gasorin
- basu • takushii • torakku • ōtobai
- bijinesu • shoppingu • sērusuman
- sēru • depāto • kurejitto kādo

PAGE 120

- bāgen • esukarētā • serufusābisu
- nyūsu • terebi • rajio • tēburu
- apāto • manshon • beddo • toire
- sūtsu • zubon • shatsu • waishatsu
- doresu • pajama • nekutai • jiipan
- burausu • sukāto • pantsu • masuku
- asupirin • uirusu • infuruenza
- arerugii • borantia • pāto
- arubaito • jaketto • sūpā
- kurisumasu • santa kurōsu • kyandē
- piano • gitā • kureyon • fasshon
- moderu • kamera • bideo • shiidii

PAGE 121

- Watakushi no apāto wa semakute kurai desu ga, tomodachi no manshon wa hirokute akarui desu.
- Supōtsu ga totemo suki desu. Beisubōru to sakkā ga daisuki desu. Tenisu mo shimasu ga, gorufu no hō ga jōzu da to omoimasu.
- Sumisu sensei wa kurasu de itsumo waishatsu to nekutai o shimasu.
- Tonari no oniisan wa depāto de hataraite imasu ga, arubaito o sagashite iru sō desu.
- Senshū atarashii konpyūta o kaimashita ga, monitā ga kowarete ita node, kinō kaeshimashita.

PAGE 122

- Mainichi oshigoto ni iku toki, basu de ikimasu ka, soretomo takushii de ikimasu ka.
- Chotto kibun ga warui desu ga, uirusu ka arerugii ka wakarimasen.
- Yōroppa ni itta toki, ōkii hoteru ni tomarimashita. Robii dake de uchi no apāto yori ōkii desu.
- Andāsonsan wa maishū nichiyōbi ni byōin de borantia o shimasu.
- Resutoran no mae ni tatte iru hito wa jonson sensei no tomodachi dewa arimasen ka.

PAGE 123

- Maishū getsuyōbi ni chikaku no resutoran de asagohan o tabemasu. Itsumo hottokēki to orenji jūsu o chūmon shimasu. Demo, ashita wa tabun sōsēji ka hamueggu ni shiyō to omoimasu. Kōhii wa nomimasen ga, jūsu ga daisuki desu.
- Kyonen kazoku to amerika e itte kimashita. Hikōki de Hawai ni itte, Honoruru ni mikkakan tomarimashita. Airando Tsuā o shite, tsugi no hi, Waikiki Biichi de asobimashita. Sorekara Rosanzerusu o keiyu shite, Rasbegasu e ikimashita. Soko no Gurando Hoteru ni tomatte, basu de tsuā o shite, yoru wa kajino to shō o tanoshimimashita.

PAGE 124

- Sakuban yūshoku o tabete, terebi no nyūsu o mimashita. Sorekara kodomo o tsurete aisukuriimu o tabe ni ikimashita. Uchi ni kaette bideo gēmu o shitari, hon o yondari shimashita. Kodomo ga neta ato, jūniji made terebi de puro resuringu o mimashita.
- Kono shashin wa kyonen no kurisumasu no toki depāto de torimashita. Kodomo o tsurete Santa Kurōsu o mi ni ikimashita. Kono betsu no shashin wa onaji hi desu ga, tomodachi no musume desu. Kanojo wa fasshon moderu desu yo. Totemo kirei na hito desu ne. Okāsan to futari de tonari no manshon ni sunde imasu.

• Kinyōbi wa watashi no tanjōbi deshita. Okāsan wa chokorēto kēki o tsukutte kuremashita. Ojiisan to obāsan ni okane o moratte, atarashii jiipan to sandaru o kaimashita. Ranchi ga owatte kara, kōen ni itte, sukēto o shimashita. Totemo ii bāsudei deshita.

• Abe: "Ken-san, shachō ga kyō ranchi o gochisō shite kuremasu ga, nani ga ii desu ka.
            Pittsa ka hanbāgā ka, dochira ga ii desu ka."
  Ken: "Chiizubāgā ga ii desu ne. Soshite poteto furai mo onegai dekimasu ka."
  Abe: "Nomimono wa ikaga desu ka."
  Ken: "Sōda ga ii desu ne."

• Uchi no shujin wa Igirisujin de, eigo mo Furansugo mo Itariyago mo hanashimasu. Watashi wa Nihon de umare-mashita ga, nisai kara Furansu ni sunde ite, Furansugo no hō ga jōzu desu. Imōto wa Furansu de umaremashita keredomo, Roshiajin to kekkon shimashita. Ano hito wa Roshiago mo Furansugo mo yoku wakarimasu.

• Depāto de bāgen sēru o shite imashita kara, kesa hayaku soko ni ikimashita. Kodomo ni pajama to pantsu o katte, watashi ni wa burausu to sukāto o kaimashita. Shujin wa sūtsu ga hitsuyō desu ga, zubon to waishatsu to nekutai shika kaimasen deshita.

Senshū gakkō ga hajimarimashita. Tonari no tomodachi wa boku to onaji rekishi no kurasu o totte imasu kara, issho ni benkyō shimasu. Kurasu ga owatte kara sugu toshokan e itte, kyōkasho o yonde, shukudai o shimasu. Atode shokudō de ranchi o tabemasu. Ichiji ni tomodachi wa eigo no kurasu e itte, boku wa sanji made kurasu ga nai node, hitori de toshokan ni modotte, benkyō o tsuzukemasu. Sūgaku no kurasu ga owatte, uchi e kaerimasu.

APPENDIX D

Translations for practice exercises and self-tests

PAGE 40
1. What is this?   2. That is a watch.   3. Who is that person?   4. She is Tanaka.   5. Is the restaurant over there?   6. Where is the lavatory?   7. He is not a teacher.   8. Is that person a foreigner?   9. The post office is over there.   10. I was a student.   11. The entrance is over there, isn't it?

PAGE 41
1. What is it?   2. Where is the library?   3. The bank is over there.   4. Where are the employees? 5. The employees are in that room.   6. Is there a wastebasket in that room?   7. There is not a desk in the classroom.   8. Who was in that room?   9. He is not [in].

PAGE 42
1. Welcome.   2. Where are you going?   3. This morning I came to school.   4. Yesterday Tanaka did not come to the office.   5. The company president returned by taxi today.   6. Are you going home already?   7. How (by means of what) did she go to Tokyo?   8. I did not go to the post office yesterday.   9. He is a friend.

PAGE 43
1. Is that person studying Japanese?   2. Please telephone the company president one more time. 3. She is not reading the newspaper.   4. Tanaka drove the car as far as the post office.   5. I went to the bookstore, but didn't buy a book.   6. Won't you please eat with me today?

PAGE 44
1. Why don't you go to the classroom?   2. Please don't phone until tomorrow.   3. Can you come again next week?   4. I am busy tonight, so I cannot go.   5. Since guests will come soon, please don't go back yet.   6. Why did older brother not eat?   7. Let's study until 11:00, okay?

PAGE 45
1. What does it mean?   2. Do you have a question?   3. Good morning.   4. Good night.   5. Is that right?   6. See you later.   7. You understand, don't you?   8. Goodbye.   9. How much is it?   10. It is $15,210.   11. It is expensive, isn't it?   12. No, it's cheap!   13. What is your name?   14. I am called Tanaka.   15. Pleased to meet you.   16. Please accept my regards.   17. Thank you very much.   18. Think nothing of it.   19. It is 960 yen.

PAGE 46
1. Where is the exit?   2. The entrance is over there, isn't it?   3. Is he not a teacher?   4. My university is in Tokyo.   5. Which one is your desk?   6. That's too bad, isn't it?   7. In the office there is both a wastebasket and a clock.   8. Which room is his?   9. In the classroom there are both teachers and students.   10. Are the company president and the employees in that room now? 11. Your car was not over there.

PAGE 47

1. Welcome. / Come in.   2. Let's go together next time.   3. Did you go to the post office last week?   4. Next week I will go home with older sister by subway every day.   5. Thank you for the meal.   6. Please wait a moment.   7. I'll be right back.   8. Mother and older sister were eating together in the restaurant.   9. He went home at fifteen minutes till ten. 10. I was waiting with Tanaka at the university exit last night.   11. Is younger brother working in Osaka?   12. Younger sister is reading a letter in [her] room now.

PAGE 48

1. Excuse me for bothering you.   2. Happy birthday.   3. Where do you always take [your] break?   4. I was not able to study all day long.   5. Please don't buy the book yet, because there is no money.   6. Can everyone [speak] Japanese? 7. Father is travelling in Japan this year.   8. Won't you please speak with the teacher at school tomorrow morning?   9. I am hungry, but cannot have dinner yet.   10. Since Monday is a holiday, we won't go to work.

PAGE 49

Tanaka:	"Is the teacher in the classroom?"
Honda:	"No, he is in the office."
Tanaka:	"Where is the office?"
Honda:	"It is over there."
Tanaka:	"Is there a wastebasket around here?"
Honda:	"The wastebasket is in that room."
Tanaka:	"Is there a lavatory, also?"
Honda:	"No, there isn't. It is in the library."
Tanaka:	"Thank you very much."

PAGE 50

Sato:	"Shall we phone your friend?"
Aki:	"He isn't in today, so please don't do it yet."
Sato:	"Yes, I understand. (It is understood.) Well, shall we go to the library?"
Aki:	"Excuse me, but I can't today, because I am busy. I'm sorry."
Sato:	"That's okay! How about tomorrow?"
Aki:	"Yes, tomorrow will be splendid!"

PAGE 51

1. Is that your book?   2. He was not a teacher.   3. The library is over there.   4. Are you not a student?   5. Which one is the post office?   6. That is her dictionary, isn't it?   7. That person's desk is over there.   8. Tanaka's watch is expensive, isn't it?   9. Those people were university students.   10. That person over there is the company president, isn't he?   11. The bookseller is a foreigner.   12. We are not Japanese people.

PAGE 52

1. Your friend is in the cafeteria now.   2. Where is the lavatory?   3. I do not have a car.   4. She was in Tokyo last week.   5. The students were not in the classroom yesterday.   6. Who is there in that room?   7. This bike is not his. 8. Both the employees and the company president are in the office.   9. Is the wastebasket also in the lavatory? 10. Those people were in the post office yesterday morning.   11. The restaurant is over there, isn't it?   12. Both the bank and the library are there.

PAGE 53

1. Are you going to the library today?   2. Last night I did not go to the cafeteria.   3. The company president went to Tokyo by plane, right?   4. Older sister returns by subway every day.   5. Last month everyone came by train. 6. Let's go by boat next year.   7. You came with older brother, didn't you?   8. I don't have time now.   9. Did your younger sister return already?   10. Did your friend return to China by plane?   11. Did your husband go to last night's meeting?   12. Tanaka will return to Sapporo tomorrow.

PAGE 54

1. What are you doing now?   2. His parents are living in Osaka.   3. She is writing a letter in [her] room.   4. Older brother and father were running together.   5. Please sit over there with your friend.   6. Everyone has returned to their homes already.   7. Won't you please study a little bit?   8. I will go to the library, but will not study.   9. Tanaka was standing over there this morning.   10. They (fem.) are still taking a break.   11. Will you please sing that song? 12. I was not working at the bank.

PAGE 55

1. Tomorrow is a holiday, so please rest.   2. Can you speak Japanese?   3. Since you are sick, please don't go to the office.   4. Can't you go to next month's meeting?   5. She cannot sing.   6. Can you wait a little more?   7. Please don't buy it, because it is expensive.   8. Why did you not go downtown?   9. There is no time, so please don't eat yet. 10. Please don't speak with friends in the classroom.   11. I don't have a car, so I will go by train.   12. He cannot speak English, so he was speaking in Japanese.

PAGE 88

1. What kind of person is Tanaka?   2. I am living in a small apartment.   3. The company president is a stylish person, isn't he?   4. Was last night's meeting late?   5. What kind of people are in this university?

PAGE 89

1. What time did Tanaka come this morning?   2. I think the company president is going to Hawaii.   3. I don't think he will wait until 8:00.   4. I think he already phoned.   5. Mother did not do the shopping yet.

PAGE 90

1. I went downtown and shopped.   2. When I go to Hawaii, I stay at a friend's house.   3. I like watching movies. 4. Mother went there [and came back].   5. I think camping is fun.

PAGE 91

1. Who is the person who is sitting over there?   2. I think I want to go to a movie tonight.   3. I think I want to study with friends.   4. Who was the person who spoke in the classroom?   5. I didn't want to do anything yesterday.

PAGE 92

1. Is it okay to speak [with you] for a moment?   2. Is it okay not to phone until tomorrow?   3. It is not okay to eat in the bookstore.   4. I have to speak with the company president.   5. I have to take (drink) medicine every day. 6. It is okay to go home already.

PAGE 93

1. Is your car big?   2. Yesterday's test was difficult.   3. Today is extremely cold.   4. Her older sister is beautiful, but she is not very easy-going, is she?   5. Tanaka is a lively person.   6. What kind of apartment do you live in? 7. It is convenient, but it is not particularly cheap.   8. She became sick this morning.   9. Father likes him, so he made him rich.   10. I had a lot of work, so it became late.   11. That child is extremely clever.

PAGE 94

1. There are both orange flowers and yellow flowers.   2. Practice makes perfect.   3. She said she likes apples. 4. I cannot do the shopping, because I don't have money.   5. I think this is not the library.   6. She said she went to Japan.   7. I went to a Tokyo department store, but did not buy anything.   8. He said that they were not eating with friends.   9. I think his Japanese is not particularly skillful.   10. What did you do today?   11. This morning I ate breakfast (a meal) and went to school.

PAGE 95

1. I didn't go with [my] friends to the restaurant, because I didn't want to eat Japanese food.   2. What time do you think you want to eat?   3. I think we have to phone by 4:00.   4. Is it okay to telephone already?   5. You have to try hard!   6. Do you think it is okay to smoke tobacco here?   7. Is it okay not to do anything?   8. It is not okay for your friend to drive.   9. Your father must come.   10. I have to study both today and tomorrow.

PAGE 96

1. When it became winter, I skied.   2. That person is Japanese and cannot [speak] English.   3. They are working with all their might.   4. The company president said he has [some] extremely important business.   5. She is truly pretty. 6. I think I want to go to a movie tonight, but won't you please go with [me]?   7. I'm looking forward to it.   8. Who is the pretty woman who is working in the post office?   9. Today I think I don't want to do anything.

PAGE 97

1. Shall we eat ice cream?   2. Yesterday's test was hard, wasn't it!   3. This apartment is not particularly convenient. 4. Please clean the apartment.   5. The orange car is mine.   6. He said Americans always eat sandwiches.   7. He went to San Francisco, but he did not go to Los Angeles.   8. When I was watching television, I ate popcorn.

PAGE 98

1. Older brother is living in New York, but he studied in France.   2. I hitchhiked up to the mountains and camped.
3. When I go to Hawaii, I stay in a Honolulu hotel.   4. Mr. White said his Spanish friend is coming next week.
5. The person reading the L.A. Times now is Mr. Smith.   6. The Hawaiian wearing the white sweater watched the movie called "Stars Wars" before coming. (watched and came)

PAGE 99

1. Tanaka is a lively person, isn't he?   2. What kind of apartment do you live in?   3. It is convenient, but it is not very big.   4. Today became hot quickly.   5. The man over there is working with all his might.   6. The meeting was not interesting at all!   7. Do you like Japanese food?   8. What is your favorite color?   9. When older brother returned home yesterday, what did he do?   10. He said the department head bought a new car.   11. I don't think she can sing. (or She doesn't think she can sing.)   12. I think he said his car is red.

PAGE 100

1. He did not go to work today.   2. I think that person did not come to the office.   3. Last night's meeting was not long and [therefore it was] good.   4. That book is not particularly interesting.   5. I went to grandfather's place Saturday.   6. She works at the university every day.   7. What do you think you want?   8. He said he needs a pencil.
9. That person said he is looking for the station.   10. I went to the bookstore and bought the book that mother requested.   11. Is it okay to go home already?   12. I have to go to school again on Monday.

PAGE 101

1. Professor Smith's older sister is living in Hawaii.   2. My camera broke (became bad).   3. I got sick because I ate a bad-tasting hamburger.   4. Is the person wearing the orange sweater your friend?   5. He is working in an American bank.   6. Tomorrow I will go to the department store and buy a Mickey Mouse watch.   7. My friend is studying in a French university.   8. I think I want to go to the supermarket when lunch is finished. (Lunch ends and I want to go to the supermarket, I think.)   9. Mother went downtown by bus.   10. Did you order steak and salad?   11. Is it okay to smoke tobacco here?   12. I went to the movie theatre and saw a movie called "Cinderella."

PAGE 102

1. That pen is $10.45, and it is expensive.   2. He is Swedish and speaks French and German.   3. Is the person who is not skiing now sick?   4. I love ice cream and eat it every day.   5. Shall we go to a snack shop and eat a sandwich?
6. Did you go [and come back] by taxi?   7. There was a sale, so Mother went to the supermarket.   8. I can't drive the car, because there is no gasoline.   9. How far (up to what page) did you read?   10. I think the person who is listening to the radio is Mexican.   11. Smith and Brown are traveling in Europe.   12. I had dinner at the hotel restaurant.

PAGE 110

- This morning it was raining a lot, but at about 12:00 it cleared up, and now there is blue sky everywhere.
- Yesterday after school was out, I went to a friend's house and was treated (feasted) to dinner.
- Tomorrow is a holiday, so shall we go somewhere?
- There are both magazines and newspapers; [so] which would you like to read?
- Because Shinjuku station is full of people, it is very lively/crowded. (…it is bustling with people.)

PAGE 111

- I wrote in my diary about having traveled by train during spring break.
- Since the company will be on break for four days from (as of) August 11, I want to go to Okinawa.
- Next month school exams start, so from now on I have to study.
- The woman wearing a red hat, in front of the elementary school, was waiting for [her] children.
- I want to write a letter to my mother, but I don't have a pencil, so would you please lend me [one]?
- When Ken (Japanese name) searched inside the box, he found two large potatoes and one carrot.

PAGE 112

- Japan's four seasons are spring and summer and fall and winter. As for spring, it rains frequently, and flowers bloom. Summer is hot, so people often head to the beach. When fall comes, the leaves of the trees turn colors. After that it gets cold, and snow falls. Which one is your favorite season?
- In the middle of our yard is a big snowman. It's one that my older brother and I made. I put an old hat on the snowman's head. A tree branch cut by my older brother became the snowman's arms. Mother took pictures for us.

PAGE 113

• My dad is a carpenter and uses hammers and saws (and the like) a lot. Mom is teaching math at the high school. My older sister is a nurse and is working at the hospital. Older brother is a college student and, in the future, wants to become a bank director. I think I would like to be an ambulance driver.

• Have you ever been to a zoo? There are various [kinds of] animals, and [so] it is an interesting place. There are both tigers and bears, also elephants and giraffes (and the like), and there are small birds and snakes, as well. My favorite (#1 liked) animal is the zebra. Next week I will go, together with my family, to the Higashiyama Zoo.

PAGE 114

• On Friday my father said, "Shall we go to the park tomorrow?" Everybody yelled, "Yes, let's go!" The next morning we all got on the train and headed for a mountain park. From the bottom of the mountain, a long stairway leads/ continues up (to the top). Having climbed for an hour, finally we arrived at the top.

• Near my home is a wide river. Beside the river there are ducks. There are two parents and five children/ducklings. Every week, on Sunday, I go to see the duck family with my older sister. We don't pester them, so the ducks don't get scared. Next Sunday we will take some food.

PAGE 115

• Yesterday I went to Grandfather's house. Grandfather is getting a little old, but I think he's a very fun person. He has an extremely old car. Grandfather and Grandmother go (for fun/for a visit) someplace by car from time to time. Yesterday the three of us went (round-trip) by car to a nearby town.

• Last week I went to Osaka by airplane. I arrived at 10:00 a.m. About 12:30 I had a meal and then there were meetings until 7:00 p.m. The next morning I returned to Tokyo. Next week I will travel again.

PAGE 116

Kenji:	"I am [so] hungry I'm about to die."
Akio:	"Ridiculous! It hasn't been but two hours since breakfast!"
Kenji:	"Actually, this morning there was no time, so I wasn't able to eat."
Akio:	"You've got a problem, haven't you? There isn't anything here now [to eat]. Do you have [any] money?"
Kenji:	"I don't have but a hundred yen."
Akio:	"That's not nearly enough, you know. Shall I lend you some money?"
Kenji:	"Yes, please."

PAGE 121

• My apartment is small/narrow and dark, but my friend's large apartment is big/wide and bright.

• I really like sports. Baseball and soccer are my favorites. I also play tennis, but I think I'm better at golf.

• Professor Smith always wears a white shirt and tie in class.

• The young man next door is working at the department store, but I hear he is looking for a second job.

• Last week I bought a new computer, but the monitor was broken, so I returned it yesterday.

PAGE 122

• When you go to work every day, do you go by bus, or do you go by taxi?

• I don't feel very well, but I don't know if it's a virus or an allergy.

• When I went to Europe, I stayed in a large hotel. The lobby alone is bigger than my apartment.

• Mr. Anderson volunteers at the hospital every Sunday.

• Isn't the person standing in front of the restaurant a friend of Professor Johnson?

PAGE 123

• On Monday every week I eat breakfast at a nearby restaurant. I always order hotcakes and orange juice. However, tomorrow I think maybe I will make it sausage or ham and eggs. I don't drink coffee, but I love juice.

• Last year I went [round-trip] to America with my family. We went to Hawaii by airplane and stayed in Honolulu for three days. We took the "Island Tour" and, the next day, played at Waikiki Beach. After that, by way of Los Angeles, we went to Las Vegas. We stayed at the Grand Hotel there, took a tour by bus, and in the evening enjoyed a casino and a show.

• Last night I ate dinner and watched the TV news. After that, taking the children with me, we went to eat ice cream. Returning home, we played video games and read books. After the children went to sleep, I watched pro wrestling until 12:00.

• I took this photo at the department store at Christmas time last year. I took the children with me to see Santa Claus. This other photo is the same day, but it is a friend's daughter. She is a fashion model! She's a very pretty person, isn't she? She lives in a large apartment next door with her mother (the two of them).

• Friday was my birthday. Mother made me a chocolate cake. I got money from Grandfather and Grandmother and bought new jeans and sandals. After lunch was over, we went to the park and skated. It was a very good birthday.

• Abe: "Ken (English name), the boss is treating us to lunch today, so what would you like? (…what is good?) Pizza or hamburger—which one is good?"

  Ken: "A cheeseburger is good. Also, can I ask for french fries, too?"

  Abe: "How about a drink?"

  Ken: "Soda is fine."

• My husband is an Englishman and speaks both English and French, as well as Italian. I was born in Japan, but having lived in France since age two, my French is better (than my Japanese). My younger sister was born in France, but she married a Russian. He (that person) understands both Russian and French well.

• There was a bargain sale at the department store, so I went there early this morning. I bought pajamas and under-wear for the children and, for myself, I bought a blouse and skirt. My husband needs a suit, but I didn't buy anything but pants and a white shirt and necktie.

School started last week. My friend next door and I are taking the same history class, so we study together. When class is over, we go immediately to the library and read the textbook and do homework. Afterwards, we eat lunch at the cafeteria. At 1:00 my friend goes to English class, and I don't have a class until 3:00, so I go back to the library by myself and continue studying. When math class is over, I return home.